DEVELOPING INTERCULTURAL AWARENESS

A Learning Module
Complete with Master Lesson Plan,
Content, Exercises,
and Handouts

Developed by
L. Robert Kohls

The Society for Intercultural Education, Training and Research
Washington, DC

First Edition
April, 1981

Copyright © 1981 by
L. Robert Kohls

Library of Congress Catalog Card No. 81-51263
ISBN 0-933-934-07-6

Manufactured in the United States of America

10 9 8 7 6 5 4 3 2 1

Table of Contents

ACKNOWLEDGEMENTS

The author wishes to express his gratitude to the following for permission to use the materials indicated:

Mobley, Luciani & Associates, for permission to use ideas contained in their Value Option Cards in the development of Cross-Cultural Value Cards (Resource 2).

Meridian House International, for permission to quote from *There IS a Difference*, by John Fieg and John Blair; copyright 1975 by Meridian House International (Resource 3).

Examples 13 through 20 in Resource 3 (Observations of Foreign Visitors About American Behavior) are from *American Education through Foreign Eyes*, edited by Anthony Scarangello; copyright 1967 by Hobbs, Dorman & Company, New York. SIETAR was unable to contact or locate Hobbs, Dorman & Company for permission to quote from this out-of-print book.

Dr. Alfred J. Kraemer, of the Human Resources Research Organization (HumRRO), Alexandria, VA, for ideas contributing to development of Kohls' list of Implicit Cultural Assumptions (Resource 6). Kraemer's work was reported in *Intercultural Sourcebook*, published for SIETAR in 1979 by the Intercultural Network, Chicago, IL. A more complete description of Kraemer's work may be found in *Development of a Cultural Self-Awareness Approach to Instruction in Intercultural Communication* (Technical Report 73-17; HumRRO, Alexandria, Viriginia, 1973).

Dr. Francis L.K. Hsu, for his comparison of American and Chinese cultural assumptions which contributed to Kohls' development of his list of Implicit Cultural Assumptions of Americans (Resource 6). This work appeared in *The Study of Literate Civilizations*, published by Holt, Rinehart & Winston, New York (now out of print).

V. Lynn Tyler, Brigham Young University, for permission to use several case studies appearing in Resource 10.

BNA Communication, Inc., for permission to use ideas on evaluation approaches which appeared in the *Bulletin on Training*, March, 1980.

FOREWORD

Let me say it as simply and as forcefully as I can: There is no more noble calling, in the last quarter of the twentieth century, than to help the people of the world live together in peace and understanding, with a fully developed spirit of inquiry about other cultures and other ways. If America has reached any degree of maturity, we have certainly come to the realization that it is time for us to learn from others as well as to teach others about our ways. This cannot be achieved as long as each group sits smugly locked inside its own ethnocentric cocoon. You can have a part in breaking cocoons and bringing about this enlightened awareness!

Many people write books to amplify and expound. I write to simplify and clarify. There is a danger inherent in my approach, however, for one can end up looking like s/he knows less than is actually the case. I am willing to take that chance.

This is a very simple book, a how-to book. It shows how to lead a workshop designed to develop intercultural awareness in a culturally naive audience. But although it is a basic how-to book, it assumes some intercultural awareness already present on the part of the facilitator. If that knowledge and understanding is not already present, the would-be facilitator should read and absorb the seven books listed in Resource 13 (p. 66) before attempting to lead a workshop like the one presented here. There is no excuse for ignorance, and if the facilitator doesn't start out with a greater knowledge of the subject than that possessed by the trainees, someone else should be the facilitator.

Many readers will recognize exercises in this book they have seen elsewhere. I have always shared my training materials with anyone I felt could make use of them, and trainers to whom I have given them have, in turn, passed them on to others. The *Intercultural Sourcebook*, published by the Intercultural Press, included several of my designs, especially the Minoria-Majoria Simulation, Reaching Consensus, the "As If" Exercise, and A Way of Getting At American Values. The reader may wonder why they are being included here if they are no longer new materials. The reason, quite simply, is that I have wanted *Developing Intercultural Awareness* to be as complete a resource as possible.

For two major activities in the accompanying Lesson Plans (pp. ix-xviii), the reader is referred to another book by the author, *Survival Kit for Overseas Living: for Americans Planning to Live and Work Abroad* (Intercultural Press: Chicago, IL: 1979). Pages 12 through 27 in the *Survival Kit* will provide the content for these two lecturettes.

I encourage the cross-cultural trainer to be as experimental and as eclectic as possible. What has worked for me may not work for you. Feel free to shift and substitute as your imagination and the circumstances of your situation dictate. There is no single right way.

Above all, have fun at it. I have !

L. Robert Kohls
Washington, DC
January, 1981

GENERAL CONSIDERATIONS
for the Learning Module
Developing Intercultural Awareness

1. Expected Audience:

Adults who may be considered to be culturally naive. This module has been successfully used with American businessmen and their spouses, military officers, teachers, graduate-level university students, Peace Corps Volunteers, Foreign Service Officers, and missionaries. In short, Americans preparing for a positive overseas experience can benefit from this module.

It has *not* been designed for multicultural audiences, nor is it intended for foreign nationals.

2. Objectives:

This module is designed to:

a. Increase your positive attitudes toward the people of other countries.

b. Increase your ability to communicate with people of other cultures.

c. Make you more aware of your own American values and unstated cultural assumptions which may make you seem strange to other national groups.

d. Reduce any counterproductive stereotypes and prejudices which you might have toward people of other cultures.

e. Prepare you to be better adjusted and more productive in an overseas living experience.

3. Materials and Resources required:

- An overhead projector and transparencies (prepared in advance)
- Screen or projectable wall surface
- Flipchart or blackboard
- Moveable chairs (to allow changing of groupings)
- Handouts as included in activities descriptions (prepared in sufficient quantity in advance)
- The Minoria-Majoria simulation (Resource 7), if used, requires the specific supplies listed on page 15.

4. Number of Participants:

This lesson plan has been used successfully with from five to sixty trainees. Obviously, different approaches must be taken for smaller or larger groups. About twenty is the most desirable group size.

5. Room Requirements:

Room size must, of course, correspond to the size of the group. Moveable chairs, which will allow multiple groupings, are an absolute requirement. Well-lit, sunny rooms have a definite psychological advantage over dark or windowless rooms.

LESSON PLAN (6 hours, with breaks)*

Time	Activity	Training Point	Handout	Overhead Transparency
5-10 mins.	*Welcome:* • Brief self introduction by Trainer	Opening Establishing credibility		
	• Presentation of Objectives (See p. vii)	"Buying into" Workshop's purpose	Workshop's Objectives	
30 mins.	*Intercultural Introductions:* • Each participant to introduce self as a cross-cultural being	Initial Activity; Individual presentations to get to know each other; Information sharing		
	• Stress any cross-cultural experience(s) you have had, any sub-cultures of which you are a member, any needs you have to improve your inter-cultural awareness	Learning the total cultural experiences and needs of the group		
	• Facilitator introduces self this way *first*, as an example	Modeling; establishing credibility		

* See pages 70-72 for additional suggested activities

LESSON PLAN (6 hours, with breaks)

Time	Activity	Training Point	Handout	Overhead Transparency
45 mins.	*Consensus Exercise:* • See Resource 1 for description • Give instructions • Individual scoring • Discussion to make changes • Record written statements within each group • Have each group report orally	Group activity; To point out falacies and biases in *all* these too commonly held attitudes (but Trainer should not reveal the fact that *all* statements need changing) To let peers do the teaching; To provide opportunity for facilitator to under-score a number of key points as they come up in discussions which accompany the oral reporting	"Agreee-Disagree Statements"	*or may put* "Agree-Disagree Statements" on an overhead transparency if you prefer
30 mins.	*Lecturette:* • Ask participants to define "Civilization" or "Civilized"	Listening; Awareness of our Ethnocentrism		"Civilization" with definition "Primitive" with definition

Civilized / Primitive

Time	Activity / Content	Objective	Materials / Notes
	• Demonstration of danger of a widespread Western concept ("Civilized"/"Primitive")	*Unlearning* a cultural prejudice	(triangle: Civilized / Primitive)
	• Culture concept • For content, pp. 12-21, *Survival Kit for Overseas Living* (see Preface for citation)	Substitution of an acceptable alternative	"Developing" CULTURE Definition(s) of "Culture" — *also may be given as handout* Attributes of "Culture" — *also may be given as handout*
20 mins.	*A relatively Bias-Free Way of Comparing and Contrasting Cultures* (The Kluckhohn Model) • See pp. 22-27 *Survival Kit for Overseas Living* for content • Explain and show where American middle class values fall • Indicate where other cultures fall	Explanation of model Awareness of appropriate (unbiased) ways to compare and contrast cultures Awareness of fundamental differences between cultures	Chart of the Kluckhohn Model and also as transparency: Chart of the Kluckhohn Model

LESSON PLAN (6 hours, with breaks)

Time	Activity	Training Point	Handout	Overhead Transparency

1 hour	*Three-tiered Case Study: American Teaching in Afghanistan*
	• Resource 8
	  • Instruct to read only first section (PCV's Viewpoint)
	  • Discuss
		Group discussion; to have a realistic experience of values in sharp contrast with our own	Case Study of "American Teaching in Afghanistan"	

	• "What's the problem?" *How many different ways can you answer that question?*	Problem analysis		
	• Possible solutions - Course of Action (Collect as many possibilities as possible.) • Probable results (and repercussions) of each "solution".	No single "right" solution to any complex situation and no easy answers		
	• Now read *"Keeper's Viewpoint"* • Now read *"Inspector's Viewpoint"* • Who is "right"?	Awareness there is more than one valid point of view (relating to very different value systems)		

- Are there any solutions which are not one extreme or other? Is a compromise possible? (e.g., obtaining old books to exchange, or convincing Keeper to check out books to students daily)
- Supplementary letter to hand out for reading (Resource 9)
- What's the problem? Share Lawrence of Arabia quote:

"That's the problem!"

"The Conflict Between Islamic and Western Values in the Classroom"

"How could I, as me, meet this new people? How would I have to change?

What of me was superficial and might be sacrificed and what need I keep to remain myself?"

30 mins.	Reactions to Observations by Foreign Visitors about Americans

- See Resource 3 for instructions.
- Divide into groups, give directions, and read quotations (assigning each one to a different group)
- Assignment: Discuss
  1. What is the issue?

Group activity; questioning why we do things the way we do

Practice explaining and defending why we do what we do; looking for the logic behind our actions

Looking at ourselves

LESSON PLAN (6 hours, with breaks)

Time	Activity	Training Point	Handout	Overhead Transparency
	2. Is the criticism *true*? *Fair*? 3. What *underlies* it? 4. How could you *explain* or *defend* it? • Report orally to whole group • Facilitator makes whatever additional points need to be made and underscores key points worth reinforcing	from a different point of view	May also give quotations as handout	
30 mins.	*Stereotypes of Americans Held by Foreigners* • Brainstorm sterotypes commonly held of Americans by Foreigners • See Resource 4 for points not to be omitted • "Easy to see why we have been called 'Ugly Americans' " • How many are *true*? *Deserved*? • Even if untrue or undeserved, or if you personally are not guilty, *you* will be blamed for them • How many are *positive* points?	Attention-getting Brainstorming Making aware of actions which are destructive and should be avoided Assuming responsibility		Duane Hanson's sculpture of "Tourists" (source: *Survival Kit for Overseas Living*, p. 4)

- Make point that most of ones we consider positive may be considered *negative* by foreigners (give examples)

- What are the sources of such stereotypes?
(American tourists, movies, TV programs, YOU?)

30 mins. *Discovering American Values*
Ask "What are American Values?"

- Difficult to answer, even though we've all been encultured as Americans

- Easy to discover--through American proverbs and axioms

- See Resource 5 for directions

- Take 5 or 10 minutes to have each write own list

- Collect on flipchart (leaving space on right)

- Together, determine what value is being taught by each, one by one

- Recommend Selwyn Gurney Champion's book, *Racial Proverbs: A Selection of the World's Proverbs Arranged Linguistically**, as rich

To make aware of American values, how difficult they are to list, even though we have all been thoroughly indoctrinated into them; and how easy it is to retrieve them through our proverbs

Other countries' proverbs can also reveal *their* values

LESSON PLAN (6 hours, with breaks)

Time	Activity	Training Point	Handout	Overhead Transparency
	source for other countries' proverbs			
10 mins.	Some American "Implicit Assumptions"	Listening		
	• So accepted they are never questioned and don't have to be verified-- we just act as if they were true beyond a doubt	Awareness of how "deep" these assumptions are		
	• The people of that culture believe that every intelligent person would also "see things that way"	Awareness that they are *not* absolutes, even though we had always assumed they were		
	• Yet all cultures' implicit cultural assumptions are quite contradictory to those of other cultures			
	• See Resource 6 for several of America's implicit cultural assumptions	Note-taking (if desired)		America's Implicit Cultural Assumptions
	• Suggest those who know another culture intimately			

(revealing points
one at a time)

	may like (on their own) to try making a similar list for that country		
10 mins.	*Suggestions for Further Reading, Extensive Bibliographies, and Area Studies Resources*	Where to go for more in-depth information	Resource 13
15 mins.	*Questions or Relevant Comments*	Questions and Answers Sharing Closure	
15 mins.	*Group's Analysis: of Main Points Covered in Workshop* • Participants, *not the* Facilitator, do the summing up • Facilitator jots ideas down on flip chart	Summary Closure	

*Barnes and Noble, New York, 1964

N.B. Many additional exercises and resources are included in the "Additional Exercises & Resources" section, pp. 70-72. Resource 10 (Additional Case Studies), pp. 27-63, contains a large number of case studies to substitute or add to your workshop.

DEVELOPING INTERCULTURAL AWARENESS

Resource 1

REACHING CONSENSUS

1. Divide the group into smaller subgroups (of 3 to 5).

2. *Individually*, place an "A" or a "D" beside each statement on the attached sheet to indicate whether you personally *agree (A)* or *disagree (D)* with it.

3. Then, going over each statement in order, check to see if *anyone* in your group disagrees with it. If even one person disagrees, the group should change the wording so that the statement is acceptable, as reworded, to *all* members of the group. The same applies when *everyone* in the group disagrees with a statement: it must be changed so as to make it acceptable.

4. You *may not* simply "agree to disagree." That's a cop-out.

5. Choose one member to record the revised, acceptable statements.

6. Report orally. Ask each group to report on a couple of the statements, and ask for alternate revisions from other groups.

7. If time is limited, it's a good idea to ask for one or two of the subgroups to start from the bottom of the list and work their way to the top, so that all the statements can be covered in a shorter time.

8. The important advantage of this exercise is not so much in the validity of the statements *per se*, but in the discussions they spark. It allows participants to learn from their more enlightened peers. This exercise also provides the facilitator with the opportunity to underscore certain key points.

ATTACHMENT TO RESOURCE 1

1. The fact that America was able to place a man on the moon proves America's technological superiority ...... ——

2. Foreigners going to live in a new country should give up their foreign ways and adapt to the new country as quickly as possible .... ——

3. Orientals do many things backwards .... ——

4. Much of the world's population does not take enough initiative to develop themselves, therefore they remain "underdeveloped" .... ——

5. English should be accepted as the universal language of the world .... ——

6. The Vietnamese do not place any value on human life. To them, life is cheap .... ——

7. Americans have been very generous in teaching other people how to do things the right way .... ——

8. Primitive people have not yet reached the higher stages of civilization .... ——

9. Minority members of any population should be expected to conform to the customs and values of the majority ... ——

10. The sooner the whole world learns to do things the way we do, the sooner all the people of the world will be able to understand each other better .... ——

Resource 2
CROSS-CULTURAL VALUE CARDS

- For a group of 15 to 50 people. (Works best with large groups.)
- Keyed to values on the Kluckhohn model (which will be explained later).
- Based on similar Value Option Cards invented by Mobley, Luciani and Associates.[1] This cross-cultural version was developed by L. Robert Kohls.
- See attached sheet for values (to be typed separately on 3" × 5" file cards, one value per card), or photocopy the values, cut the boxes apart, and paste them on file cards, one per card.

1. Facilitator passes out four cards at random to each person as they enter the room. One "set" is fifteen cards. (Prepare enough duplicates to have a total of four cards per person.)

2. Participants are instructed to trade their cards to *upgrade* them. Each participants must end with no fewer than two cards (this means you may trade more than one card for one you particularly want).

3. Pair up with other members of the group whose values are *compatible* with your own. Discuss what you have in common.

4. Facilitator then disbands former groups and instructs them to join together, in pairs, with another person whose values are directly *opposite* to their own. Assignment: Prepare a joint compromise statement with which both members are in agreement.

---

[1] Value Option Cards invented by Mobley, Luciani & Associates, 16 West Sixteenth Street, New York, NY 10011.

ATTACHMENT TO RESOURCE 2

MOST PEOPLES CAN'T BE TRUSTED.	THERE ARE BOTH EVIL PEOPLE AND GOOD PEOPLE IN THE WORLD AND YOU HAVE TO CHECK PEOPLE OUT TO FIND OUT WHICH THEY ARE.	MOST PEOPLE ARE BASICALLY PRETTY GOOD AT HEART.
LIFE IS LARGELY DETERMINED BY EXTERNAL FORCES, SUCH AS GOD, FATE, OR GENETICS. A PERSON CAN'T SURPASS THE CONDITIONS LIFE HAS SET.	MAN SHOULD, IN EVERY WAY, LIVE IN COMPLETE HARMONY WITH NATURE.	MAN'S CHALLENGE IS TO CONQUER AND CONTROL NATURE. EVERYTHING FROM AIR CONDITIONING TO THE "GREEN REVOLUTION" HAS RESULTED FROM OUR HAVING MET THIS CHALLENGE.
MAN SHOULD LEARN FROM HISTORY AND ATTEMPT TO EMULATE THE GLORIOUS AGES OF THE PAST.	THE PRESENT MOMENT IS EVERYTHING. LET'S MAKE THE MOST OF IT. DON'T WORRY ABOUT TOMORROW: ENJOY TODAY.	PLANNING AND GOALSETTING MAKE IT POSSIBLE FOR MAN TO ACCOMPLISH MIRACLES. A LITTLE SACRIFICE TODAY WILL BRING A BETTER TOMORROW.
IT'S ENOUGH TO JUST "BE". IT'S NOT NECESSARY TO ACCOMPLISH GREAT THINGS IN LIFE TO FEEL YOUR LIFE HAS BEEN WORTHWHILE.	MAN'S MAIN PURPOSE FOR BEING PLACED ON THIS EARTH IS FOR OUR OWN INNER DEVELOPMENT.	IF PEOPLE WORK HARD AND APPLY THEMSELVES FULLY, THEIR EFFORTS WILL BE REWARDED.
SOME PEOPLE ARE BORN TO LEAD OTHERS. THERE ARE "LEADERS" AND THERE ARE "FOLLOWERS" IN THIS WORLD.	WHENEVER I HAVE A SERIOUS PROBLEM, I LIKE TO GET THE ADVICE OF MY FAMILY OR CLOSE FRIENDS IN HOW BEST TO SOLVE IT.	ALL PEOPLE SHOULD HAVE EQUAL RIGHTS, AND WE SHOULD ALL HAVE COMPLETE CONTROL OVER OUR OWN DESTINY.

Resource 3

OBSERVATIONS OF FOREIGN VISITORS
ABOUT AMERICAN BEHAVIOR

- Observations are taken from actual observations made by real foreigners about America. They are not fabricated.
- Examples 1 through 17 are quotations collected by John P. Fieg and John G. Blair in *There IS a Difference: Seventeen Intercultural Perspectives.*[2]
- Examples 18 through 30 are from *American Education Through Foreign Eyes*, edited by Anthony Scarangello.[3]

1. Divide the group into subgroups of 3 or 4.

2. Read quotations aloud to all groups, assigning each statement to a different group as you read it aloud. A larger-than-necessary number of quotations is presented here so that the facilitator may be selective in choosing ones which particularly appeal to him/her.

3. Assignment: *Discuss*

    a. What is the issue?
    b. Is the criticism true? Fair?
    c. What underlies it? (Get at the *logic* behind it.)
    d. How could you *explain* or *defend* it?

4. Report orally to the whole group.

QUOTATIONS OF FOREIGN VISITORS

1. *Visitor from India:*
   "Americans seem to be in a perpetual hurry. Just watch the way they walk down the street. They never allow themselves the leisure to enjoy life; there are too many things to do...."

2. *Visitor from Japan:*
   "Family life in the U.S. seems harsh and unfeeling compared to the close ties in our country. Americans don't seem to care for their elderly parents."

3. *Visitor from Kenya:*
   "Americans appear to us rather distant. They are not really as close to other people—even fellow Americans—as Americans

---

[2] Fieg, J.P. and Blair, J.G. *There IS a Difference: Seventeen Intercultural Perspectives.* Meridian House International, Washington, DC: 1975.

[3] Scarangello, A. (Ed.) *American Education Through Foreign Eyes.* Hobbs, Dorman & Company, New York: 1967.

overseas tend to portray... it's like building a wall. Unless you ask an American a question, he will not even look at you... individualism is very high."

4. *Visitor from Turkey:*
   "Once... in a rural area in the middle of nowhere, we saw an American come to a stop sign. Though he could see in both directions for miles and no traffic was coming, he still stopped!"

5. *Visitor from Colombia:*
   "The tendency in the U.S. to think that life is only work hits you in the face. Work seems to be the one motivation...."

6. *Visitor from Indonesia:*
   "The atmosphere at a sorority party looks very intimate, but if the same people met on the street, they might just ignore one another. Americans look warm, but when a relationship starts to become personal, they try to avoid it."

7. *Visitor from Indonesia:*
   "In the U.S. everything has to be talked about and analyzed. Even the littlest thing has to be 'Why? Why? Why?. I get a headache from such persistent questions. I still can't stand a hard-hitting argument."

8. *Visitor from Ethiopia:*
   "The American seems very explicit; he wants a 'Yes' or 'No' —if someone tries to speak figuratively, the American is confused."

9. *Visitor from Ethiopia:*
   "Trying to establish an interpersonal relationship in the U.S. is like trying to negotiate over or break down a wall; it is almost like a series of concentric circles. You have to break down different levels before you become friends."

10. *Visitor from Iran:*
    "It is puzzling when Americans apply the word 'friend' to acquaintances from almost every sector of one's past or present life, without necessarily implying close ties or inseparable bonds."

11. *Visitor from Iran:*
    "The first time my professor told me: 'I don't know the answer— I will have to look it up,' I was shocked. I asked myself, 'Why is he teaching me?' In my country a professor would give a wrong answer rather than admit ignorance."

12. *Visitor from Iran:*
    "To place an aged or senile parent in a nursing home is appalling for our people; taking care of one's parents is the children's duty. Only primitive tribes send their old and infirm off to die alone!"

13. *Visitor from Indonesia:*
"The [American] wife of my English professor in Indonesia once asked me why I never invited her to my house. I frankly could not give her a direct answer. There was no reason why I should invite her since there were no parties being held by my family, or if she really wanted to come to the house, she was always welcome at any time. I know now that in America you cannot come freely to any place unless you are invited."

14. *Visitor from Indonesia:*
"The questions Americans ask me are sometimes very embarrassing, like whether I have ever seen a camera. Most of them consider themselves the most highly civilized people. Why? Because they are accustomed to technical inventions. Consequently, they think that people living in bamboo houses or having customs different from theirs are primitive and backward."

15. *Visitor from Indonesia:*
"I was so surprised and confused when on leaving Whittier Hall, the provost, in person, held the door for me in order to let me pass before he would enter the door. I was so confused that I could not find the words to express my gratefulness, and I almost fell on my knees as I would certainly do back home. A man who is by far my superior is holding the door for me, a mere student and a nobody."

16. *Visitor from Indonesia:*
"In America, people show hospitality to strangers, but do not care for family members."

17. *Visitor from Hong Kong:*
"In my family where I stayed for the weekend, I was surprised to see the servant eating with the children and calling the children by their Christian names."

18. *Visitor from Australia:*
"I am impressed by the fact that American teachers never seem to stop going to school themselves."

19. *Visitor from Vietnam:*
"Americans are handy people (even the women). They do almost everything in the house by themselves, from painting walls and doors to putting glass in their windows. Most of them showed me the pretty tables and bookshelves they made by themselves in their spare time."

20. *Visitor from Kenya:*
"In American schools, the children are restless, inattentive, and rebellious" [and the teachers have] "poor class discipline."

21.   *Visitor from Kenya:*
"Parents are so occupied earning the weekly or monthly pay that they find very little time to devote to their children."

22.   *Visitor from Kenya:*
"...there is very widespread neglect of respect which children ought to give to adults [in the U.S.]."

*23.   *Visitor from the Philippines:*
"They say children everywhere are the same. In my observations I found out a couple of ways where children differ. Children in the United States are very forward in their way of speaking, even to their parents and elders. Children here show a lack of respect for old age. Also, I have observed that children here do not offer their services to their parents willingly. They either have to be told what is to be done or they have to be given some reward or compensation for what they do."

24.   *Visitor from the Philippines:*
"In the United States I have observed that the mother is the dominant parent in most families."

25.   *Visitor from Algeria:*
"I was horrified at the ignorance of the high school students about my country—Algeria. They knew nothing at all about it—location, people, language, political condition. What made it worse was the ignorance of the teacher herself. Her knowledge was very shallow and, in certain instances, quite erroneous."

26.   *Visitor from Japan:*
"Unfortunately, I have been given a bad impression by some American students who speak of their own country very badly, especially of its foreign policy. I knew all the foreign policy of America isn't good, but I did not want to be told so by a native. I hate people who speak badly of their own land, even if they speak the truth."

27.   *Visitor from Japan:*
"There is much more freedom of speech in Japan than in America, because we cannot speak about communism in America. I have found out that American people are so much afraid of Russia, even though they are propagandizing their superiority over Russia."

28.   *Visitor from Korea:*
"In a twelfth-grade social studies class, the teacher gave choices of assignment for the next class. I didn't like the idea of pupils choosing the assignment. I wonder what these pupils will do later in life when there are no choices in the duty assigned to

them. They must learn while they are in school how to do well the jobs assigned to them from above."

29. *Visitor from Afghanistan:*

"I was so much surprised by the many people in America who were under special diet to lose their weight. In our society we are in search of food in order to gain weight."

30. *Visitor from Egypt:*

"My hostess asked me, 'Would you like to settle down in our country for good?' She was surprised when my answer was in the negative, though I took great pains to make it as diplomatic as possible."

Resource 4

MOST COMMON STEREOTYPES OF AMERICANS HELD BY FOREIGNERS

- Outgoing, Friendly
- Informal
- Loud, Rude, Boastful, Immature
- Hard working
- Extravagent, Wasteful
- Think they have all the answers
- Not class conscious
- Disrespectful of authority
- Racially prejudiced
- Know little about other countries
- All American women are promiscuous
- All wealthy
- Generous
- Many hippies
- Always in a hurry

This is by no means a complete list. Add your own.

Resource 5

DISCOVERING AMERICAN VALUES
THROUGH AMERICAN PROVERBS

1. Write on the blackboard or flip chart:
   - Cleanliness is next to godliness.
   - Time is money.
   - A woman's place is in the home.[4]
   - Little children should be seen and not heard.

2. Ask everyone in the group to take 10 to 15 minutes to write down all the American axioms and proverbs they have heard over and over again. (If any foreign students are in the group, have them do the same for their countries.)

3. Then share and collect by writing on the blackboard or flip chart.

4. Then, next to each axiom, determine (as a group) what *value* is being taught.

Examples:	Values:
Cleanliness is next to godliness.	Cleanliness.
Time is money.	Value of time; time thriftiness.
A penny saved is a penny earned.	Thriftiness.
Birds of a feather flock together.	Guilt through association.
Don't cry over spilt milk.	Practicality.
Waste not; want not.	Frugality.
Early to bed, early to rise....	Diligence.
God helps them who help themselves.	Initiative.
It's not whether you win or lose....	Good sportmanship.
A man's home is his castle.	Privacy; private property.
No rest for the wicked.	Guilt; work ethic.
You've made your bed; now sleep in it.	Responsibility.

These are only a few, very random examples. The list is endless, but the point has been made. With only a dozen or so axioms, you have a pretty good list of American values being expressed.

You might want to have the group brainstorm other basic American values that are not on the list.

---

[4] This is intended to be provocative.

Resource 6

IMPLICIT CULTURAL ASSUMPTIONS OF AMERICANS

"Implicit cultural assumptions" are those beliefs which lie so deep in any culture that they are never questioned, stated, or defended. They are simply taken as "givens" which any intelligent, cultured individual anywhere could accept. Needless to say, every intelligent, cultured individual *doesn't* accept all of *our* implicit cultural assumptions. In fact, many, even most, of the world's people operate on their own implicit cultural assumptions which are most likely 180° at variance with ours. (It is surprising how *un*-American seven-eighths of the world is!)

This list draws heavily upon the work of Alfred J. Kraemer of the Human Resources Research Organization (HumRRO).[5] I am also indebted to Francis L.K. Hsu for his work in the field, especially for his excellent comparison of American and Chinese cultural assumptions in *The Study of Literate Societies*.[6] *Managing Cultural Differences* by Philips R. Harris and Robert T. Moran[7] includes several other implicit cultural assumptions of Americans, some of which you may wish to incorporate into the abbreviated list which follows:

- No Belief in Fate — Instead: Personal Control of the Environment
- Change Seen as Inevitable and Desirable
- Equality/Egalitarianism
- Individualism
- Self-Help Concept.
- Competition and Free Enterprise
- Future Orientation
- Action Orientation
- Informality
- Directness and Openness
- Practicality
- Materialism.
- Problem-Solving Orientation
- "Cause-and-Effect" Logic

---

[5] As reported in Hoopes, D.S. and Ventura, P. (Eds.) *Intercultural Sourcebook*, SIETAR/Intercultural Network, 70 West Hubbard Street, Chicago, IL: 1979.

[6] Hsu, F.L.K. *The Study of Literate Civilizations*. Holt, Rinehart & Winston, New York: 1969 (out of print).

[7] Harris, P.R. and Moran, R.T. *Managing Cultural Differences*. Gulf Publishing Company, Houston, TX: 1979. pp. 46-47, Table 4-1, "U.S. Values and Possible Alternatives."

Resource 7

MINORIA—MAJORIA SIMULATION

(Developed by Tad Erlich, L. Robert Kohls,
Margo Kiely, and Bill Hoffman)

• Large group simulation (up to 60).

1. Divide the group into two halves. Give each group *separate* briefings (see scenarios). Don't let the groups hear each other's scenario until the debriefing, following the simulation.

2. Minorians wear black crepe paper armbands for identification; Majorians wear white crepe paper armbands.

3. Materials:

Minorians	Majorians
(given only minimal supplies)	(given luxurious materials)
Newsprint (or old newspapers)	Colored crepe paper
Brass fasteners	Colored tissue paper
String	Paper doilies
	Scotch tape
	Masking tape
	Scissors (representing
	technical superiority)

4. After the simulation: *debriefing* and *discussion* to process the experience.

5. Derobing Ceremony (to break out of roles and end any hostility caused by the simulation): All participants rip off their armbands and throw them into a common wastebasket. (This is absolutely essential.)

INSTRUCTIONS TO MINORIANS

You are residents of the country of *Minoria*. Minoria is not a new country but a very old one with a noble history and a rich culture. Unfortunately, your country has been dominated by other nations for so long that you are just now beginning to regain a sense of independence and pride. You have finally been able to shake yourself free of those countries which had dominated you and exploited you for so long, and you have a great jealousy of your hard-won freedom to run your own country the way you want to.

Unfortunately, one of the problems that besets you is the fact that you have few natural resources, and because you have been dominated by others for so long, you have not been able to develop the ones you have nor the technology to make use of them. Poverty is a problem in your country, but it is one you have learned to live with and even to accept as the normal way of life.

This is the anniversary of your independence, and you are searching for some appropriate focus around which the new national pride can develop: a monument, symbol, or something similar. Your task is to begin discussing what kind of monument will best symbolize that pride and then to construct it with the materials and resources you have at hand. You want, partly out of pride, to use your own native materials to the extent possible, but also because you do not have the money to import materials, and, too, because you do not want to become indebted to outsiders. You are especially wary of gifts with political strings attached.

You have just received word from the Ministry that in the next twenty minutes a team of people will be arriving from a country called Majoria. Although you have never had an opportunity to meet any Majorians, Majoria is well known to you, since it is one of the leading countries in the world. Its resources seem to be endless. While you are pleased for suggestions and appreciative of help, you resist any type of patronizing and you are anxious to do your own thing. Other nations have dominated you for centuries and you are suspicious of Trojan horses.

After twenty minutes of planning, you will have no more than thirty minutes to execute the plans you have made. On with your monument! Long live Minoria!

INSTRUCTIONS TO MAJORIANS

You are the fortunate citizens of Majoria. Majoria's technology, natural resources, and wealth make it a country without peers in the modern world. Your people have solved the scourges of earlier centuries: epidemics, hunger, limited production, illiteracy, etc. People in your country worry little about survival, and more about opportunity in a land of abundance.

Unfortunately, there are other countries that are far less

fortunate. Many people in your country are concerned about their plight. Some out of guilt of having so much while others have so little. Others out of the realization that the world will not long be safe if the imbalance of technology, resources, and materials continues. Because of your genuine concern for less fortunate people and your idealism, you have volunteered to go to an obscure little country named *Minoria*.

Minoria is a poor, underdeveloped nation. Side by side there are the contrasts: affluence and want, the handsome leaders and the starving beggers, new buildings and shacks without sanitation, the bespectacled professor and the illiterate country people. Behind the plush front, the statistics of hunger, disease and unemployment tell the real story. *Minoria* is new among the world's nations and its leaders, policy makers and technicians are inexperienced at their work. Frequently, things are done on the merest whim and have no relation to the country's basic needs.

Minoria needs many things. It is struggling to survive in the modern world. Many fear it will not. Its primary need is firm insistence on an ordering of priorities to place the few resources where the greatest needs lie. Second, the country needs other resources to supplement its own. Third, they need the technical help to make sure what they construct endures, and what they have will be used well.

You have ten minutes[8] to plan what you will to do to help before arriving in that country. After your arrival, you will be expected to help them plan a major project that will benefit their country, and to help execute that plan using the materials you have at hand.

Remember, you will be evaluated on your ability to:

a. Help them reset priorities which match their needs;

b. Help them use the materials you have brought wisely;

c. Make helpful construction hints and give technical aid on the decided project.

---

[8] Note to Trainer: This discrepancy with the "twenty minutes" indicated in "Instructions to Minorians" is intentional. The Majorians are to arrive ten minutes before the Minorians are expecting them.

Resource 8

CASE STUDIES:
AN AMERICAN TEACHING IN AFGHANISTAN
(Developed by Rosalind Pearson and others
for the U.S. Peace Corps)

FROM THE PEACE CORPS VOLUNTEER'S VIEWPOINT:

My seventh grade class had no books. Nearly every day at various times for eight weeks, I went to the storeroom where the supply of books was kept. Each time I was told that the keeper was out, and that no one else, not even the principal, had a key. I gradually began to visualize this "keeper of the keys" as a mythic man of giant proportions. But, one day, he actually appeared at the storeroom—a wrinkled little man in a gray turban.

I told him that I needed 120 ALE Book One's for my seventh grade classes. I could see the books piled in neat, but dusty stacks on the shelves. He looked at me in a puzzled way. "Where are your books?" he asked. Thinking that he had not understood me, I said, "No, you don't understand. I do not have books. That is why I am here. I need to get books for my three seventh grade classes. I need 120 books."

"No, no," he said, standing firmly in the doorway. "I cannot give you books unless you give me books. I am responsible for the books in this room. I am a very honest man. If I give you the books then I won't have any books, and how will I explain an empty storeroom that was given to me full of books?"

I tried to be patient with the old man. But I had to make him understand the necessity of my getting the books.

I had worked orally with my students all this time, but, each day they asked me, "Where are our books, *maalem sayb?*" They were eager to have them, particularly since all the upper classes had books. I had tried various ways of writing out exercises for Book One as I had remembered them, but the school had no duplicating machine, and this meant writing out 120 papers by hand.

The government was most anxious to start to distribute the textbooks all over the country in an attempt to standardize the English classes. The Peace Corps was a vital part of this effort. It was even harder to accept the fact that because I was unable to get books for my classes, I was going against the goals set by the Peace Corps and the Ministry.

When my kids went on to the eighth grade, they would be poorly prepared indeed, if they had never worked with an ALE text, never learned to read from a printed page (students have a hard time making the jump from handprinted to type-printed words).

I was responsible for teaching these boys and I owed them my best efforts. What would I have given them if, at the end of the year, they didn't know how to read and they were unprepared for the work of the next grade?

The most frustrating part of all this was that the books were there in the very same building as my students. The books were sitting in the storeroom waiting to be used, and my students were sitting in the classroom waiting to use them. All that stood between the books and the students was a locked door and an illiterate old man with the key to open it.

The storekeeper was unable to accept my reasoning, was unmoved by my pleading, and when I told him I would take all the responsibility for the books, and promised that every book would be back in place at the end of the year, he merely laughed as if he thought I was mad. He could never understand that not using the books was the same as not having them.

I went to the principal to see if he could intervene on my behalf, but there was nothing he could do since he had no key, and the Inspector from the Ministry would probably not come for several months.

Time was passing, and I was getting more and more desperate. I talked and talked to the keeper, but he remained invincible.

We could have had a thousand PCV teachers in this country, but if there was a keeper behind each one of them, nothing would be accomplished. I don't see how this country is ever going to progress if everything is kept locked up to rust and mold. It's enough to make you give up and go home. I finally wrote to the Peace Corps office. Maybe they can do something about this.

FROM THE KEEPER'S VIEWPOINT:

It is not every day that an old man like me has the honor of being appointed to a Government job. The people of my village are very poor, and we have much difficulty in our lives. I will do this job well, and the Government will, perhaps, look with favor upon my son. Our people are used to hardship. My many years of life have seen many evils, and have given me some knowledge of the ways of men. If it be the will of Allah, I shall do my work well and bring honor to my family.

Truly it is a great responsibility for me to be entrusted with the room of many fine books. I have not seen such books before in my life. Even though I must travel a great distance from my village to the school, I am proud to do so. Certainly, this school is a very fine school to have so many books.

There is the man named Nasratulian, from the Ministry of Education in the capital city, who comes to the school during the year to look at the storeroom. He is an important man with a high position, and it is my great honor to please him. Should he take a good report of my work to the Ministry, it will be very fortunate for my son, my family, and my people. It is great pleasure for me to see in my lifetime such things come to pass, Allah be praised!

There are some things in my work that, with my humble background, are difficult for me to understand. How can I explain to the young and impatient man from America about my position? He has very strange ideas. He does not understand that these boys will lose the books. They are well-meaning boys, but they are mischievous. When the Inspector comes to see the books, and finds that the books are not here, I will have to pay for them, and how am I to do that? What shame it would be for my family! What should Nasratulian Khan think of me when he finds that some of these valuable books are lost?

And what should he think if he comes to see his humble friend, Kurban Ali, and finds instead the young man from America sitting by the storeroom with the key?

He would think, "Oh, that old man has gone back to the mountain. These people are not suited for such work, as I had suspected all along." That would indeed be a terrible thing. I would disgrace my family; my son would have to be content to farm; his children would be unhappy. No, such a thing will not occur. By the guidance of Allah, I am a good and honest man, and I will live up to the responsibility given to me.

I do not understand what that young man says about his students. I know his students, and they are very content with him. He is indeed a strange person. Imagine, a man from America becoming a Keeper of Books! That is truly a strange idea. He seems unhappy here—such a village must be difficult for him. In America, villages are very large. Perhaps his unhappiness makes him discontent with our people.

He does not understand that my responsibility is to make sure that nothing happens to these books. He wants me to have an empty storeroom! What should I do if I had no books to look after?

Each time I come, I count the books, and make sure they are neatly stacked. Each time all the books have been counted, and I have not lost one book. This is my responsibility. How can a baker make bread with no flour?

FROM THE INSPECTOR'S VIEWPOINT

It is very difficult to deal with these people who keep our storerooms. They have little understanding, no education, and cannot be trusted. One must be very firm with them, or else there would be all kinds of dishonesty and corruption. It is my responsibility to see that such corruption does not occur. I have forty villages to inspect throughout this Province—indeed, a great responsibility.

I must keep my eye on old Kurban Ali—he is the newest storekeeper in the District and, as they say, a new servant can catch a running deer, but he is only of a low caste and his family is poor. Those people must be watched because we cannot expect very much from them. He could make a lot of extra money by selling the books, if I do not watch him.

Also, many new supplies were sent to that school, and it is necessary to make sure that they do not get misplaced. The Ministry has been able to increase the production of textbooks, much to the benefit of our country, and we must see that every school in the entire Province has the new English books.

I am very careful to keep records of what has been given to the schools in my District. At the beginning of the year, we supplied a total of 1,300 books to the schools. Each time I go to school, I must make sure that none of the books has been misplaced. The people in the smaller villages are ignorant, and do not know how to take care of books, and we must teach them the value of having these books.

I know only too well how difficult it is to make the students understand this. As soon as they get the books, they sell them in the bazaar and they become lost. They leave them outside and they become dirty. They make marks in them with their pens. Therefore, it is important to make sure that the fine books printed by the Ministry are not lost or ruined, for it will be a long time before we get others.

It is necessary for me to be very firm with the Bookkeepers, and to make sure that they pay for any books they lose because of their carelessness or irresponsibility. If the Keepers in my District lose books, or become subject to bribes, it is because I have not been firm enough with them.

How will I explain lazy Keepers in my District? How can I write my report and say that we gave out 1,300 books at the beginning of the year, and at the end of the year there are only 1,200? Truly, this is not good for me. The Ministry has given very direct instructions to all Inspectors not to tolerate lazy or irresponsible Keepers in our Districts. It is necessary for our country to develop responsible people.

Resource 9

THE CONFLICT BETWEEN ISLAMIC AND WESTERN VALUES IN THE CLASSROOM[9]

Sometimes I'm convinced that I've been teaching English in this little Moslem town too long for my own good.

The whole social structure of this country tends to undermine the goals of the Western scholar. Logical thought processes, on which most Western teachers rely instinctively, have just never been taught here. Deductive reasoning is unheard of. The teacher is thought of only as a lecturer and a recorder; what he teaches is not original; it has been true from the beginning of time and known since the time of Mohammed. The teacher has made no discoveries of his own and will make none; but, as he has been fortunate enough to have been taught, he is in turn priviledged to re-teach what he has learned. As truth is unchanging, there is nothing to discuss or question. The teaching process is a continuation of the oral tradition; what has been learned in the past is now transmitted verbatim to the student who writes it down and then memorizes it. This method, however, is more than tradition: it is dictated by the nature of the cosmos and can only be the repetition of what Allah revealed to Mohammed, the last and greatest of Allah's prophets. There is no other way of knowing. As original knowledge does not exist, the most reliable way to learn is through the same medium and by the same technique that knowledge has been acquired in the past.

Accordingly, there is no discussion and no personal opinion in the Moslem classroom. The teacher either reads to the students from his notes, or from a book, and they copy in their notebooks what is read to them. Sometimes a student is substituted for the teacher and he reads to the boys. No papers of any kind are ever written, and there is no questioning the teacher. To these people there is only one truth; the idea that two "experts" might interpret the same facts in opposite ways is inconceivable to them. An American teacher once "proved" to his class that 1 equalled 2. No one objected, and the students all wrote the proof down in their notebooks. The teacher had shown it to them; therefore, it must be true. There is no distrusting the conveyor of the source of truth.

In this society it is the form, and not the content, that is important, and herein lies the most significant problem that the Western teacher has to deal with. In the Moslem scale of values it is not so important that a student cannot know seventeen subjects at

---

[9] Source unknown, but this is an authentic letter from an American who had spent approximately two years in an Arab country.

once, as long as the curriculum makes it look like he is learning them. It is not so important that the students have a high rate of absenteeism as long as the books show full attendance [the same is true of teacher attendance.] Thus, the passing grade of 35%, though in reality showing an inferior knowledge of the subject, is in practice considered adequate. A boy with 70% knowledge is considered very good. The student himself does not feel that learning itself is important; what is important to him is the card that shows the teacher has given him a passing grade. [The common concept is that the teacher *gives* you a grade; you do not earn it]. This is not to say, of course, that the same phenomena do not exist elsewhere; it is to say only that they predominate almost without exception in this country. A boy with a 35% to 50% grade in the United States, for example, does not kid himself that he has learned very much, and indeed may consider, with regret, that he missed a good opportunity to learn. Here the question of learning or not learning rarely comes into mind.

A concomitant problem is the one of cheating in the classroom. There is rarely a test of any kind given during which cheating does not occur, for in the Moslem classroom it is almost literally true that it is sufficient for only one student to understand the lesson. One of the five pillars of Islam is alms-giving, the aid one gives to those whom Allah has made less fortunate. The concept of alms-giving pervades all aspects of life. Thus, cheating, and by extension bribing, nepotism, etc., are not looked at as being morally wrong as they are in the Western world; in fact, in many cases they are considered laudable acts. To the Moslem, it is an obvious fact that Allah has made some people more intelligent than others, and, in a sense, classroom performance is pre-ordained; there is no feeling that hard work may enable one to pass by his own efforts, make him a better person, etc.; there is only the feeling that, unaided, many will fail, and that it is thus a duty to pass on knowledge to the less fortunate ones. In fact, the teachers themselves aid and abet the cheating by lax observation during exams, for a good class record reflects favorably on their abilities as teachers!

Unfortunately, cheating does not only occur on exams, but also on a day-to-day classroom basis. On this level, it is a mechanism to "save face." When the teacher calls on a student, he is expected to know something. In most cases it is recitation of some kind that is required. Usually the student listens to a student behind him who, with open book, is reading him the answer. By this means of prompting, a student may go a whole year without the teacher ever realizing that in reality he knows nothing. Homework is usually ineffective because the students refuse to struggle with it. Instead, another student or a brother or relative will do it. Behind these external manifestations we again find different values. Actual gains are subordinated to surface appearances.

Intrinsically related to this network of social and religious values is their attitude toward individual effort. It must be pointed out here that their attitude is a realistic one in terms of their culture, yet one which the Western teacher reacts against and must cope with. Life is tough in the Middle East; a lot of work often means little or no change. Thus, sometime in the past, in order to better live with themselves and the harsh world around them, these people came to feel that individual effort, in most cases, comes to naught. In reality, in this part of the world, effort does not count; it is Allah who determines what is or is not to be achieved.

Essentially this means that the end rather than the means is of value, while to the Westerner, more often than not, it is the other way around. Again, it is the problem of the form being more important than the content. As mentioned previously, there is no feeling in the classroom that hard work and proper questions—in short, an all-out effort to understand instead of memorize—might bring about some kind of good, either in grades or in other, less tangible ways. Many of the students are capable, and willing, to do hard work, but feel it worthwhile only in the drudging path of learning by rote, which they are used to. It is the hard work of *thinking* that they balk at, the work of understanding that A plus B does not equal A plus B, but equals C, a third object that has to be deduced, not memorized.

What must be emphasized is that many of these above-mentioned values make sense in terms of the society and are wrong only as far as they conflict with Western values as possessed by the Western teacher. For a Western teacher to feel he is accomplishing something he must to some extent instill his own values in his students, for they are the only things he can measure by. What is hard for him to face is the degree to which these American values do not and cannot pervade Moslem life and the realization of the chances against his success. When he realizes that his students are never face-to-face with any other than their country's values, except, perhaps, in that forty minutes a day he is teaching English, he is bound to feel he is fighting a losing battle. He sees that he cannot afford to teach only English, he must go beyond this to create attitudes and values which are exactly opposite. The student sees from his father that hard work and individual effort count for little, while he sees from his uncle that cheating and bribing do lead to the top. He knows that being a relative of nobility is far more important than being intelligent, and he knows that the boy next to him will pass because his father is an important man. Therefore, he might as well show his paper to him and retain a friend. In the long run, it is he, and not the Western teacher who knows how things are done and who will succeed and not succeed.

The greatest problem comes when the Western teacher begins to see the logic of Islamic values. He begins to doubt himself and becomes too sympathetic to the plight of his students. He is in danger of being half Easternized himself.

Resource 10

ADDITIONAL CASE STUDIES

Country: Afghanistan

Issue: Favoritism vs. Ethical Considerations

Source: *Discussion Leader's Manual for Cross Cultural Studies Training: Afghanistan.* Prepared by Rosalind Pearson and Janet Bing. Peace Corps.

You are a teacher in Kabul. The son of your principal is attending Habibia, the most prestigious high school in the country, and the son of the principal of Habibia is attending your school and is, in fact, in your class. He is a poor student and it is obvious to you and his classmates that he is failing English miserably. You have consistently warned the class that you will pass only those who know their English and will show no favoritism in grades. Most of the students gradually have come to believe this and are finally working hard. There has been, you have noticed, less cheating on homework and quizzes, and you considered this a good indication that they have finally begun to see the worth of individual achievement.

One day your principal comes to you and asks you to pass the Habibia principal's son, since the principal of Habibia is doing a similar favor for his son there. You want to continue your good working relationship with your principal and yet you do not want to betray your own values. How will you handle the situation?

Country: Afghanistan

Issue: Concept of Hospitality and Sharing

Source: *Discussion Leader's Manual for Cross Cultural Studies Training: Afghanistan.* Prepared by Rosalind Pearson and Janet Bing. Peace Corps.

Najiba appeared at our gate one Friday morning during Jeshen. She was a good friend of mine but I usually went to her house since she was rarely on our side of town. This was the first time that she had come to our house alone. It was already getting on toward late afternoon and we were going to Jeshen that evening to see all the lights and fireworks. We asked her to come along but she said she was meeting a friend there and would just ride with us.

So we sat around for a while and drank tea and looked at magazines. Since Friday was the cook's day off and there was literally nothing in the kitchen except a couple of eggs, some sugar and a little tea, we had planned to go out to eat—either over to the house of some other Volunteer or to the Khyber Restaurant.

We finally got around to leaving and my husband said: "Why don't we wander over to the girls' house—we can have something to eat over there." Normally, I would have agreed, since we often stopped in and vice versa. They had a big household and there was always room for more at the dinner table. But under the circumstances, with Najiba in tow, I didn't think much of the idea but obviously, in front of Najiba, I couldn't say why, and my husband was insistent, so off we went.

Well, everyone was already at the table. One of the girls came out and we introduced Najiba. Then my husband simply asked her outright if they had enough for us to eat and the girls said they were having chicken. If it had just been two of us we probably would have stayed, but having to obviously cut pieces in half and stretch things in front of Najiba would have been awkward and probably would have made her embarrassed. In any case, the girls said that they really didn't have enough—maybe for two but not really for three extra people, so without hesitation, my husband said, "Okay. Just thought we'd stop by." He'd gotten the direct answer he required, but no sooner had we left the compound when Najiba turned to us and asked, "Why did they say there wasn't enough? I thought they were your friends."

We explained that they were our friends but that since they had not been expecting us, they didn't have enough food prepared for us.

"But, I don't understand; an Afghan would never say he didn't have enough. Even if there was only one egg, they would share it. And if there was nothing, they would go out and buy something. And if they had no money to buy, they would borrow. Not enough! I can't believe it." Then she started to laugh uncertainly as if there must have been some kind of joke she wasn't quite understanding, but I think she really felt that we had all been greatly insulted. We didn't act insulted, though, and she probably tried to laugh to cover up her own uncertain feelings.

We went on to the fellows' apartment, since we were planning to go to Jeshen with them and when we went upstairs, Najiba probably thought we were going to eat dinner there. We managed to get some tea together, and after that we all went to the Khyber Restaurant to eat. Najiba didn't say anything during all of this—she was totally bewildered and had obviously resigned herself to keeping quiet and just following us from place to place.

Several weeks later when I saw her again, she asked me to come to her house for dinner. I said I would love to and then she hesitated and said, "But do you mind if just you come and not your husband, because we don't have enough chairs. It's all right to say this, isn't it?"

Country: Afghanistan

Issue: Cultural Differences in the Division of Labor

Source: *Discusion Leader's Manual for Cross Cultural Studies Training: Afghanistan.* Prepared by Rosalind Pearson and Janet Bing. Peace Corps.

We had a rather violent argument with our servant Nasim over who was to shovel the snow off the roof after the first snowfall. We told him to do it first thing, even before going to market, since the longer it sits the more it seeps into the mud roof, and eventually the roof will collapse. When we went outside to go to school, there was a hired coolie on the roof shoveling. Nasim told us that shoveling snow was coolie's work and that we were to pay the coolie 30 afs. We were furious, not only because 30 afs was way too much (Nasim was probably planning to pocket the difference) but because we had told Nasim to do it himself, that it was part of his job. Nasim refused to go up on the roof and he just stood there watching the coolie do all the work. My husband told the coolie to leave; he grabbed the shovel himself and climbed up on the roof while Nasim still stood below and looked most uncomfortable. After finishing about half the roof, we had to leave for school, and my husband told Nasim firmly that he must finish the job himself and that we were not going to give him money for a coolie. We hadn't even gone halfway down the block before the coolie was up on the roof again. Nasim would rather pay for the coolie out of his own pocket, I guess, than to do the work himself. His last puzzling words as we went out the gate were, "Sayb, who shovels the snow off your roof in America?"

Country: Afghanistan

Issue: Who is Expected to Pay?

Source: *Discussion Leader's Manual for Cross Cultural Studies Training: Afghanistan.* Prepared by Rosalind Pearson and Janet Bing. Peace Corps.

This Afghan guy was in my history class and I thought it would be a good idea to speak to him once in a while as he didn't seem to have too many friends. So after class one day, I went up to him and asked him how he liked the class and a bunch of other questions, just to get going. He seemed very eager to talk—even though he didn't say much, and, as he didn't seem eager to hurry off to anything, I suggested that we go off to the Den for some coffee. He agreed right away, so we went out and got on this bus that goes around campus for a nickel, because the Den was on the other side of campus, a couple of miles away. I dropped my nickel in and headed for a seat, but the Afghan didn't follow me right away. I turned around and saw him standing at the fare box looking around uncertainly and fumbling in his pockets with about ten students behind him waiting to get on the bus. The driver was getting annoyed but the guy didn't seem to have any luck finding a nickel, so I went up and explained that he was supposed to put a nickel in the box, since it occured to me that he might not know what to do. The driver was getting more and more impatient and I didn't think it would be so hot if he started yelling, so I put a nickel in for him figuring he could pay me back later. He seemed very relieved. When we got to the Den I ordered a sandwich with my coffee and he did the same. We talked about this and that, and when the checks came, he didn't pick his up. Well, okay, but I was glad we hadn't gone to the delicatessen where it's considerably more expensive. It also became clear that he had forgotten about the bus fare. Funny—he didn't even say "thank you" or anything when he left, although he certainly seemed to enjoy himself. After all, I did end up treating him.

Country: Afghanistan

Issue: Bribery and Legality

Source: *Discussion Leader's Manual for Cross Cultural Studies Training: Afghanistan.* Prepared by Rosalind Reason and Janet Bing. Peace Corps.

About 11:00 on the morning of April 25th, I was proceeding from Shar Nau to Karte Char in the Peace Corps jeep with a Peace Corps Volunteer. I was reducing speed at the intersection near Baghe

Alimadon in preparation to making a right turn there. As I began the turn, a car began to honk its horn behind me, and a VW appeared beside me still honking and made a half circle around me, attempting to also make a right turn from my left side. There were people standing at the corner to my right side near the curb, and I moved in that direction, but the VW rubbed its right rear fender against the spare tire on that side (the left side). The Volunteer and I were not aware that something had happened when the VW dropped back alongside us and Mr. Ayub, the VW driver, began waving threateningly at us. With him in close pursuit I continued to the police station at the Damazang Circle where the Volunteer and I went into the police office. Mr. Ayub soon appeared too. We were told that another station handled incidents in the area of the accident, so we followed Mr. Ayub to the other station. He crossed two lanes of traffic in the same manner he had crossed in front of me en route, and we went through a red traffic light as well.

When we arrived at the station and Mr. Ayub had explained his case in Persian, the officer on duty told me to pay Mr. Ayub 300 afs. I asked him to call an official from the American Embassy, at least as a translator, but he declined to do this.

I then began to make plans with the Volunteer for him to go and bring someone from either the Peace Corps or the Embassy to the station. At that point we were permitted to make a telephone call. I called the Peace Corps office and talked with the Deputy Director who arranged to have Mr. Harrison and Mr. Zia from the Embassy meet us at the station.

When they arrived, I was given a hearing with Mr. Harrison presenting the details of the accident as they clearly had happened. There were no official or even quasi-official proceedings as far as I could tell, though Mr. Harrison continually asked to be confronted with the proper officials. It became apparent that the station officer was going to regard his original decision as the final judgment, yet we were never presented with a notice of violation of the law or a written request for payment. The official stated that we could ask for formal proceedings only after an estimate of damage was made, the judgment to be made on the basis of costs involved.

Mr. Harrison suggested that we could not do better, in all likelihood, than to pay the *baksheesh* (tip or bribe), but he did not oppose my asking for a formal settlement of the affair. This would seem to me to be the appropriate course in terms of discharging our official obligation to the Afghan legal system and certainly in line with the Peace Corps goal (as I interpret it) of being an example of upright, above-board dealing. I am not anxious to become a part of the *baksheesh* method of government. Mr. Harrison left the decision to me, and I chose to ask for a legal solution and not a *baksheesh*-shakedown. The Embassy personnel departed.

The traffic official, Mr. Ayub, and I went into the station office. Inside, the official indicated that Mr. Ayub could leave but that I was to remain. I suggested that we were both involved and that I felt that I, too, should be allowed to make arrangements for my case. He agreed that we should be treated equally, and he dispatched a policeman to go with Mr. Ayub and me to get an estimate for the repair of Mr. Ayub's car. Since Mr. Ayub had contended that the jeep had struck him with its front fender (and there is a dent there) I suggested that the repair costs of the jeep be estimated, too. After some discussion, most of which I did not understand, we all went to get an estimate for the repair of the jeep. Mr. Ayub convinced the shopmen at Indamer that they should not make an estimate on this damage, and they would not. At the Kandahary shop he was less successful, but the repairmen did produce a bill for 20 afs. I asked him if he really would repair the fender for that small amount he had written down if I brought the jeep in next week. He then changed the figure to 200 afs, and I think he would have added another zero if I had told him we would bring it in for sure. Subsequently, Mr. Ayub dropped the account that the front fender had struck him. It really was an old dent.

A long harangue followed when we returned to the traffic office and a higher official was there to review the whole thing. I had even more trouble understanding his Farsi, but it was clear that he was resting his case on the fact that I had not stopped at the intersection where the accident had occurred. I asked him simply if it were a violation of the Afghan laws and if he could tell me the penalty. He said it was an infraction and that it would cost me between 500 and 1,000 afs. I was questioned about my employment before I was given this figure, and I explained that I worked for the Peace Corps and that it was a Peace Corps vehicle. I said I would pay this or any appropriate fine for violation of driving regulations. I inquired if the turn and the position of the vehicle in the turn was illegal. He did not say that it was illegal and did not quote a fine for this. He began to insist that I was at fault in the accident and that I must pay Mr. Ayub, but he wanted to reduce my payment to about 200 afs. I restated that I would see that the fines which he imposed would be paid. He pointed out to me many times that the amount of the *baksheesh* was less than the fine he could charge me, and indeed it was. I tried to make clear that I was only interested in paying legitimate charges and that I would pay a legal settlement in settling with Mr. Ayub. They did not seem to understand the difference, and an officer went out and brought back an Afghan who spoke English to explain to me that I should pay the amounts and not bother with anything more. The amounts at that stage of the bargaining were 700 to Mr. Ayub and 50 afs to the policeman.

Mr. Ayub had maintained that I was overtaking him in the intersection and the focus of the discussion turned to that point. The police official mentioned that another policeman had witnessed the accident and agreed with Mr. Ayub. I said that if a policeman had witnessed the accident and would confirm this, I would abide by the new testimony.

The Afghan translator who had come in then questioned me about my presence in Afghanistan and I explained to him that I worked with the Peace Corps. He happened to be a sports fan and was impressed with the success of the Peace Corps-coached girls' team at Aisha Duranni.

Mr. Ayub had been a soccer star and so the conversation became very friendly and turned to the friendship between the U.S. and the Afghans. The Afghan translator was very impressed with the Peace Corps and he apparently suggested to Mr. Ayub that he drop the 700 afs charge, and he would pay the 50 afs to the police himself.

I believe Mr. Zia of the American Embassy came in during the discussion, most of which I could not follow. During this part of the meeting, I was questioned as to why I didn't pay the smaller amount to Mr. Ayub, since I would not agree to let the Afghan pay the police. I told them that I didn't have the money to pay either Mr. Ayub 700 afs or the police 1,000 afs. I did have 50 afs if that amount was to settle matters, and I produced it and handed it to the police officer. Everyone seemed pleased except me. This did not decide anyone's legal rights and upset the whole purpose of my resistance. I attempted to explain (Mr. Zia had left at this point), and the police officer apparently understood and agreed with me. They were amused by it. I asked what the 50 afs was to accomplish, whereupon the officer shook my hand and returned it to me. Mr. Ayub and I shook hands, the Afghan translator mumbled some platitudes about America and Afghanistan, everyone looked embarrassed and the meeting concluded with the calm of a New England Sabbath.

Country: Brazil

Issue: American Women in Foreign Countries, Dating, Reputation

Source: Westinghouse Learning Corporation: *Manual for Use In Preparing Peace Corps Volunteers to Serve in Minas Gerias, Brazil.*

Carol, upon her arrival in Conversa, lived a few weeks in the hotel, in spite of the horrible conditions. Then she moved to a temporary room with a widow, and then finally moved in with a family.

Immediately upon arrival, full of enthusiasm, she began to get to know her town. She and her partner, Bob, visited the schools, the hospital, the health post, the various influential people in town, ACAR, and so on. They also made a point of visiting the stores, the post office, the bank, and the telephone office, talking to people and getting to know as many people as possible. Carol and Bob went to many of the rural communities together to meet the people and become acquainted with the conditions.

One day one of the more educated men in town asked Carol why her mother let her come to Brazil alone. Carol was surprised, but exlained she had been living away from home since she began studying at the university, so it was nothing too different. His only comment was that his daughter (age 25, single) wouldn't be allowed to go even five kilometers outside of town if she couldn't stay with relatives. Carol paid little attention, thinking him only an exceptionally protective parent. On various occasions, Bob and Carol were asked about dating in the United States, courting, and morals, which they explained as best they could with their limited Portuguese. The movie "Where the Boys Are" came to town about two months after Carol and Bob had been there, and they were peppered with questions for at least a week afterward. Often men, passing in the street, would call out "I love you," or "Hi, baby," and Carol would laugh and continue on her way.

Carol had always enjoyed talking with men, finding their conversations interesting and stimulating; in Brazil this was even more true since the women concentrated on gossip, usually about people she didn't know, and babies which she didn't have. As a result, she frequently found herself the only woman in a group of four or five men at parties or while making visits.

Carol ate her meals at a restaurant where food was served family style at big tables. She always ate with her partner and often other men joined them, usually traveling salesmen and bus drivers. She felt this was not a good situation but her family refused to serve her meals, principally because the woman had no maid and feared Carol would not like the food, and there was no other restaurant in town.

The main entertainment in town was the movies, so frequently Carol and her Brazilian counterpart, a girl about her own age would go. Since Carol had no fear of the dark, she would usually walk her counterpart home. She knew she was breaking a social custom returning home alone, but if she didn't do this, neither of them could go to the movies because there were no other young people in that area of town to go with them.

One day Carol needed to go to the Peace Corps office to pick up some supplies, so she told her family and they seemed surprised when she said she would be traveling alone, but she assured them they needn't worry, she wouldn't have any problems.

The fifth month Bob and Carol and their counterparts were ready to inaugurate their first Clube Agricola in one of the rural communities. They decided to have a big festival, including games, a "chunasco" and a dance in the evening. All the important people in the county were invited. Bob and Carol were very pleased and surprised to find that most of these people accepted the invitation. At lunch, Carol found herself sitting opposite Sr. Carlos, one of the richest men in town and very influential. They began to talk, and Carol was really excited to find herself able to explain her ideas adequately in Portuguese. Before she realized it, the dance had begun, and Sr. Carlos (married) asked for the privilege of dancing one dance with the charming young American, even though she protested that she hadn't yet learned to samba.

The one dance over, Carol stayed a bit longer, then she, her partner, and her counterpart returned to the city, gloating over the success of the inauguration and, especially, over the interest shown by various important people from the city.

About four days later, a good friend of the Volunteers who worked in the mayor's office came to the office and asked to speak to Carol. He then proceeded to tell her that the "gentleman" with whom she had spoken and danced with at the inauguration had spread all over Conversa, especially among the more influential people, the following tale: he had gone to the inauguration simply to try to seduce the American, and he had succeeded. She had promised to move to his house, presumably so she could tutor his children in English; she was now his mistress, and she had promised to take him back to the United States with her and travel with him for at least a year as his own private guide.

Carol asked her counterpart if she had heard this story, and the counterpart said she had. In fact, she said her family had forbidden her to go any place with Carol because of Carol's reputation.

Country: Dominican Republic

Issue: Cultural Difference in the Concepts of Giving, Charity, and Begging

Source: *Guidelines for Peace Corps Cross-Cultural Training.* Albert R. Wight and Mary Anne Hammons. Office of Training Support, Peace Corps, Washington, D.C. Published by Center for Research and Education, Estes Park, Colorado. 1970.

Whenever beggars approach me on the street holding out their hands, or touching me lightly on the elbow and murmuring "regalme algo," I tell them, "No." It has troubled me for some time that even after a year in this country, such encounters irk me enormously.

Once a Dominican friend asked me why I never gave. I explained that to give only encouraged begging and that the whole concept of begging is demeaning to a person and a nation, and that it reduced the capacity of either one to deal with his own problems. "Anyway," I said, "if I did give, people would never stop asking." He just shrugged, but I realized that he thought I was cheap. After all, begging is a part of the culture. They don't ask me because I am an American, but because they believe that I have money—they ask all rich people—it's a mark of respect. Dominicans usually do give something.

So, despite the fact that it runs counter to all I believe, I've decided to give from now on when I am asked by a beggar in the street.

Country: Dominican Republic

Issue: Male-Female Relationships

Source: *Guidelines for Peace Corps Cross-Cultural Training.* Albert R. Wight and Mary Anne Hammons. Office of Training Support, Peace Corps, Washington, D.C. Published by Center for Research and Education, Estes Park, Colorado, 1970.

I have been working here for about a month. On the whole, I'd say my relationships with Dominicans are pretty good, except for some of the men here. The are really persistent when they take a fancy to a girl.

Antonio Perez is the son of one of the more prominent men in town. He is a short, pudgy fellow—rather unattractive. Last week I was having a beer with another girl in the cafe when he came over and sat down with us. He started in right away asking me all kinds of stupid questions and talking in this low, romantic voice and making big eyes at me. Like a fool, I answered him. The next day he appeared at the hospital where I was working and hung aroung trying to talk to me until the doctor finally came out.

On Wednesday night, he showed up at my door. I was pretty surprised, because I was really cold to him at the hospital. I didn't have the nerve to be rude, but I did say I was very busy. He didn't take the hint and stood outside the house telling me how pretty I was and how he had fallen for me at first sight. He laid it on pretty thick and got rather friendly—tried to take my hand and so forth. At that point I told him I was engaged to a guy in the United States and wasn't interested. I finally got rid of him, but I practically had to slam the door in his face.

However, last night he was here again on the doorstep and this time he had a present for me. It was one of the latest Bolero records. He told me I had to take it as a token of his love. I thanked him and refused the gift, as I knew if I accepted it, he would never leave me alone. I also explained that my boy friend didn't like me to take presents from other men.

"But no," he persisted, "You must accept this. I want nothing but your friendship."

He went on and on and I, in turn, found my patience wearing thin. Finally, I told him firmly that I couldn't accept the record and thanked him very much and wished him goodnight. But he still refused to take "no" for an answer and said he wouldn't leave until I took it. So I took the record and said I was going to throw it away. At that point he grabbed me and said passionately that I must take it and he was not leaving until I said "yes."

That really did it. I was so fed up I took that record and broke it over my knee. I don't think he expected such a strong reaction on my part because he got this really angry expression on his face and left. You can bet he won't be back here soon. You really have to be firm with these men to get a point across.

Country: Ethiopia

Issue: Cultural Differences in Expectations as to How One Should Act

Source: Unknown

The school day ended. Tired Miss Larson took her classroom problems home with her and shared her concerns with friends at an informal cocktail party, shared her frustrations over teaching in the

Ethiopian government school: "For three years, I've tried to get those dear little girls to behave like normal human beings, to have some pride, to hold up their heads, look me in the face, and answer a question in a voice I can hear without straining. They're so bright; they learn as fast as the children back home, but they're hopeless, absolutely hopeless. They just can't seem to learn to behave with human dignity. For all the good I've done here, I might as well have stayed home in Iowa and continued to teach there."

The school day ended. Kebedetch walked stiffly home. The strange steel she had forced into her neck muscles seemed to have spread throughout her body. She felt rigid, brave, and frightened. Entering the gojo (small house or hut), Kebedetch was greeted warmly. Father asked the usual, daily question. "What did you learn in school today?"

Kebedetch threw back her head, looked her father in the eye, and proclaimed in a loud, clear voice, "Ethiopia is composed of twelve provinces, plus the federated state of Eritrea."

Mama and Papa talked late that night. What had happened to Kebedetch? She was no longer behaving as a normal human being. "Did you notice how she threw back her head like a man?," asked Papa; "What has happened to her shyness as a woman?" "And her voice," added Mama, "how happy I am that our parents were not present to hear a daughter of ours speak with the voice of a foreigner."

"She showed no modesty; she seemed to feel no pride. If she were normal, she would be ashamed to raise her head like that, being a girl child, and to speak so loud as that," Papa added with a deep sigh.

"Kebedetch has learned so much," said Mama; "she knows more than I, and this has given me great joy. But if her learnings are making her a strange, ungentle, beast-like person, I do not want her to learn more; she is my only daughter."

Papa pondered. Finally he shook his head and spoke. "You are right, Mebrat, our daughter must not return to school. The new education is good, but only the strongest can survive. I had hoped Kebedetch could learn and remain normal and gentle, could become a woman of dignity. This frightening behavior of hers tonight has convinced me. She has lost her sense of pride, lost her sense of shame, lost her dignity. She must never return to the school. We shall try to help her find herself again."

Country: France
Issue: Privacy and Personal Matters

Source: Brigham Young University, Language and Intercultural Research Center, Communication Learning Aid, 1977

Since Mr. Williams was assigned indefinitely to the Paris branch, he wanted to establish some social relationships with fellow employees. He had been in France only a few days when he was asked to attend a meeting in the outer office; a Mr. Baudin entered and sat beside him.

Williams politely introduced himself and they shook hands. After exchanging some pleasantries about the weather, Williams told Mr. Baudin how thrilled he and his family were to be in Paris. He casually asked how many children Mr. Baudin had. Baudin replied that he had two sons. But Williams noted that when he asked further about Baudin's family, the Frenchman seemed offended, and the conversation ended abruptly.

Williams wondered what he had done wrong. "Maybe he just doesn't like Americans," he thought. "I wish these Frenchmen would give me a chance to show them what a friendly guy I really am."

Country: Guatemala

Issue: Latin American Etiquette, Courtesy, Tact and Diplomacy vs. American Directness, Openness, and Frankness

Source: Brigham Young University, Language & Intercultural Research Center, Communication Learning Aid, 1977.

Beth sat on the bed and soaked her hot, aching feet in a basin. "I'm pooped!" she groaned, as Vickie, her roommate on the tour, stumbled from the dressing room and collapsed in the chair with a sigh.

"Me too!" Vickie exclaimed. "I love all these great ruins and things, but wow! All those steps...!"

"Oh, no! Look!" Vickie groaned. As she picked up her dusty shoe, the heel hung at a twisted angle. "The only other shoes I have are dressy. I can't wear them for the rest of the tour."

"Well, maybe when we get into Guatemala City you can find somebody to fix it for you," suggested Beth. "We'll be there Thursday."

"That's a great idea. I guess I can suffer with the patent leather for a day or two."

. . . .

Later, in Guatemala City:

Beth and Vickie turned the corner and there was the shoe

repair shop. The map drawn by the hotel clerk had been easy to follow. Behind the counter of the small shop, a man was busy replacing the sole of a boot. He stood up as they entered.

Vickie explained, in her best Spanish, that she needed the heel repaired as soon as possible. "When can you have it finished?' she asked.

"When do you need it?" the man inquired politely.

"Well, we're in the city for only a short time. I'd really like to get it back tomorrow morning. Can you finish it by then?"

The man examined the shoe carefully. "Sure," he said with a smile. "I can have it ready by then." ·

. . . .

The Next Morning:

"But you promised!" Vickie moaned,, as she looked at her shoe sitting on the shelf where the shoe repairman had placed it the day before. "You said you'd have it done this morning! If you had told me you couldn't do it, I could have looked for someone else to do it."

"I'm sorry, Miss," the repairman apologized, "but I just couldn't get to it. I'll have it done this afternoon. Please come back this afternoon."

. . . .

Later That Day:

Vickie clutched her shoe, neatly wrapped in grey paper, as she strode angrily back to the hotel. "I wouldn't be so mad," she fumed, "if he hadn't *told* me he'd do it in the first place."

Beth was sympathetic. "And look—it's nearly four o'clock. He said, 'Come back this afternoon,' but even then we sat for half an hour before he had it finished."

"I wouldn't be so mad," repeated Vickie as they entered the hotel lobby, "if he hadn't *told* me he'd have it done when I needed it. Why didn't he tell me right off that he couldn't get to it till this afternoon?"

Country:	India
Issue:	Work Value Differences; Volunteerism
Source:	*The Volunteer and the Bureaucrat: Case Studies From India.* Training Manual for India Volunteers. Vol. B. Prepared by Allen Bradford, India II Peace Corps

When I arrived on the scene, my supervisor had absolutely no idea what I was supposed to do. I wasn't sure exactly what I was supposed to do either.

The man was very hospitable. However, he had the attitude that I should just sit around and talk and drink tea and enjoy the two years. Because of this, it's a good thing he was transferred. I'd tell him I wanted to start some project, and he'd talk me out of it.

People constantly were asking me, "How much are you making?" I'd tell them, "I'm making $55 a month, which is about 400 rupees." Then they would want to know, "How much could you make in the United States?" "$500," I'd say. "Well, why did you come here?" "I came here because I wanted to. I'm a Volunteer." Then they would give me their "ah-ha" look.

The intensity may vary, but they all have their suspicions about us. They don't understand why I've come. They think I'm here for some ulterior motive.

Country: India

Issue: Understanding Another Culture's Values Only By Understanding a Message Through One's Own Experiences and Values

Source: Unknown

"Mother, wait a minute," Judy said. Something had been troubling her ever since she first came from school. "What would you say if...?" I set the plates back on the table and sat down. "What would you say if I told you I was going to become a Hindu?"

It was a good thing that I had sat down. "What did you say, Judy?" I stalled.

"What would you say if I told you I was going to become a Hindu?" She did not take her eyes off my face.

"You're not joking?" I knew she wasn't. Her deep brown eyes could not have been more serious.

"I am not joking," she said.

What was there for me to say? I had said it all so many times that I had thought the question would never arise. The sweet, earnest, devout child before me, flesh of my flesh, a Hindu! I had never thought of her in any way except a child of Christ. I had failed her, and I had failed God. I had failed the other missionaries, and our Indian Christians. How could I face anybody? All this came over me in a flash, and I was then more deeply shamed in the realization that almost my first reaction was one of loss of face.

She let me sit in silence until the whole impact of what she had said sunk in. I saw her whole life before me...her marriage... Where was Fred? Perhaps, he would be able to cope with this.

I must have looked very stricken, for she suddenly said, "I'm sorry, Mother. I just want you to know how Rani's mother will feel. Rani is going to tell her mother, this vacation, that she is going to become a Christian. When I think how close our family has been, it makes me hurt all over."

Country: Japan

Issue: Forcing a Decision; Loss of Face

Source: Brigham Young University, Language & Intercultural Research Center, Communication Learning Aid, 1977

Bob was in charge of a task force at work. He wanted to organize the others who would assist him. He visited with each one to see if they could attend an orientation meeting after work. Mr. Tanaka seemed reluctant and mentioned he wasn't sure if he could make it or not.

"Now, Mr. Tanaka, this is very important. Will you be at the meeting?" Bob asked.

Tanaka smiled and said that he would come if he could.

"Come, Tanaka," Bob persisted. "You're a bachelor and surely you can spare a few minutes. What are you doing after work that's so important?"

Tanaka was silent.

"Don't tell me you can't change your plans. This is really important," Bob continued. "You'll be there, won't you?"

Tanaka came to the meeting all right, but Bob noticed that thereafter he avoided him and arranged to deliver any messages through intermediaries. Bob was confused. "I wonder why Tanaka keeps avoiding me," he thought. "He's holding up his end of the project all right, but I wonder what rubbed him the wrong way?"

Country: Japan

Issue: Position and Age Take Preference Over Knowledge of Subject; Loss of Face

Source: USICA In-House Case Study, U.S. International Communication Agency, Washington, D.C.

A USICA research team recently conducted a successful survey of three Agency magazines in Tokyo. The contracted research company was a Gallup affiliate in Japan. The Project Director for this USICA-funded activity was the Gallup affiliate's Director of International Operations, a very prestigious position in Japan. The Director's English, while generally acceptable in written form, is very poor in conversation. The junior colleague assigned to the project has an excellent command of English, both in written and oral form. The Junior colleague also seams to have a friendlier, more open manner in working with Americans.

In meetings of the entire team, composed of both Japanese and Americans, the junior colleague tends to speak very little. He seems reluctant to offer his ideas, even though they are generally quite creative. The Project Director speaks a great deal, but his English is barely understandable and his ideas seem "tired" and bureaucratic. Although his spoken English is really inadequate, he feels he does not need an interpreter. When spoken to in English, he fakes comprehension, even though it is obvious to the Americans, from his inappropriate responses, that he doesn't know what's going on in English much of the time.

The VOA (Voice of America radio station) has become very interested in the work which the Japanese affiliate of Gallup has been carrying on in the area of Japanese public opinion of Americans. VOA program planners were impressed with the description of the affiliate's activities which they had received from the affiliate's Director of International Operations. (They did not know, at the time, that the description had been written by the junior colleague.)

You, a junior officer with USICA, have been asked to help set up an interview which will be used on an upcoming VOA breakfast show. The time scheduled for the interview is very tight, and the interviewer wants to present the best possible program. You realize it is important for the Project Director not to lose face and for the junior colleague not to upstage the Director, but you, too, are anxious that the interview be as effectiive as possible.

The PAO (Public Affairs Officer, head USICA officer at post) and the American Ambassador have both expressed keen interest in this project. They recognize the problems, and they are willing to help in any way they can. What "plan of attack" will you suggest?

Country: Korea

Issue: Role Inequality; Forcing Payment; Status of Women

Source: From a Compilation of Peace Corps Volunteer Case Studies for Korea. Peace Corps.

Part I

When I first came to Korea I had no real grasp of the place of women in the society. In training I had heard a great deal about it...but perhaps you have to experience something like that before you really understand. My expectations did not approach the facts of the situation.

When we first arrived in our province both the boys and we girls had difficulty maintaining our volunteer standing. Gifts and money were being pushed at us from everyone who wanted our help. The first refusal and explanation usually convinced most. However, our provincial board of education was tireless in finding ways to give us money. In the guise of "travel reimbursements" they would try to pay us thousands of won. We explained, pleaded, and finally refused completely to accept anything.

It was at this point in one relationship with the board that I had my most serious run-in with my co-teacher.

My deficiency in the Korean language made me dependent on Mr. Lee in some situations. I was very uncomfortable because he seemed to be exploiting the situation. He opened my account at the bank and helped me with my biographical information for the school. He used these opportunities to find out my former salary and my job. I later discovered that was not "necessary background information."

When people came to see me at school I had no interpreter but Mr. Lee. He carried on interviews as if I weren't present. I had other friends translate newspaper interviews I had supposedly given.

I became very wary and guarded around Mr. Lee. I knew that anything that hurt me would hurt Mr. Lee much more. He was the sole teacher responsible for me. I knew my best interest and his were the same. But I was very suspicious.

On this particular morning, Mr. Lee rushed to my desk and said the office needed my seal. I asked why they needed it. He replied that he didn't know exactly but there were papers that had to have my seal. I should have gone myself, but I was busy so I handed Mr. Lee my seal. He returned moments later with 2,400 won, and an explanation. The money was a padded "payment" from the board and now that my seal was on the paper I had signed for it. Mr. Lee, well aware of our quarrel with the board, laughed at my anger and the "little joke" he had put over on me.

After this incident I had as little to do with Mr. Lee as possible. I scrupulously kept him out of my affairs. He was offended and probably a little confused by this.

Part II

After the new semester began, Mr. Lee was transferred to another school. After he left, I learned that he had done much to help me during my first month of teaching. Much of the enthusiasm for my conversation class was enthusiasm he had generated for me. The motivation of the older classes was motivation he had stimulated.

Looking back I can understand his actions a little better. He could not offer me friendship because friendship only exists between equals. We weren't equals—I was a girl—and a young un-married one at that. So he could not approach me directly in any situation. He needed to use deceptive means in dealing with me to keep his conception of what the relationship should be. He needed to keep abreast and ahead of the "news" about me—so he found out what he could through deception. He couldn't converse with me as an equal. He needed to make it clear that it was he who ran me and not I who ran him—so he couldn't interpret for me. It was easier to trick me into actions like accepting the money than trying to persuade me to take it as he would have had to do in his role as co-teacher.

There are many things Mr. Lee and I could have shared had we been friends. We could have learned much from each other. The "status of women" got in the way.

Country: Korea

Issue: Cultural Differences in Social Roles, Marriage Roles, and Sex Roles

Source: From a compilation of Peace Corps Volunteer Case Studies in Korea. Peace Corps.

Soon after we arrived at our assignment, my husband, as a teacher went on the fall picnic. The students scattered along the mountainside to sing and joke, and the teachers retired to a small house to get "stoned". At this point, my husband was introduced to the Korean custom of exchanging wine cups. As a newcomer, he was the prime target for exchanges, and not knowing how to refuse without offending, and also eager to show his drinking superiority, my husband drank more than his share.

Not long after, the situation was repeated after an athletic contest at his school and his fellow teachers began calling him a famous drunkard. He realized this wasn't quite the image he wanted to have and didn't like Korean wine that much anyway, so suddenly he curbed his drinking activities.

During this time my husband's co-teachers in his department were regularly inviting us as a couple out to dinner. I was the only woman present, and though we repeatedly asked them to bring their wives with them, it remained so. After two such occasions, we became the object of their jokes—my husband was "hen-pecked" because he stopped drinking so much and didn't like to go out during the week drinking with the boys, and I was the domineering American wife who controlled her husband and refused to stay at home. We became quite uncomfortable, and when the teachers had apparently had their fun, their invitations suddenly ceased.

Since then, my husband is not invited by the men teachers to go drinking because they know he doesn't like to just drink for its own sake and that we prefer to do things as a couple. My fellow female teachers have thus far excluded my husband, although admittedly language difficulties play a part.

As a result, our only Korean social companions have become our language tutors—a Korean couple our age, well-educated. (He has been to the United States.) They are extremely unusual as they enjoy going to dinner, the movies, and parties as a couple.

Country: Libya

Issue: Difficulties American Couples May Face in Their Relationship with Host Country Nationals

Source: Unknown

After about two weeks in Benghazi, I was pleasantly surprised to meet a new friend. The owner of the Stationary Shop opposite the school, Sayyid Ben Alim, spoke rather good English and was extremely friendly. He explained that he thought highly of the Peace Corps and would like to help me in any way possible, perhaps through Arabic lessons. Not wanting to receive something for nothing, I suggested that we exchange English lessons for Arabic lessons. I said that perhaps my wife Susan would like to join us. We arranged to meet at our apartment at 1:00 p.m. the following Friday.

Sayyid Ben Alim arrived punctually at 1:00 p.m. the next Friday. I offered him tea. "Perhaps I would have a Pepsi Cola instead. You see, I like very much American things." We talked about English and Arabic for a few minutes until he suggested we start the lesson. "But where is your wife Susan? Does she not want to learn Arabic?" I told him she was a little "under the weather" and would probably join our class next week. Ben Alim seemed surprised, but the lesson went well and we parted on good terms.

Next week at 1:00 p.m. Sayyid Ben Alim arrived. I offered him tea again. "Tea, yes, we Libyans like tea, but we also like to learn the customs of our friends. We must strive to be more modern." I agreed with him and he continued: "Many of us are not the slaves of old traditions...we dress like you do, we drink alcohol, and we mix freely with women." I answered that this must sometimes be difficult in the face of their society's customs and the laws against Muslims drinking. "Yes, but we have American friends who give us beer and wine, and we make favors for them in return." I answered, "If we had any beer now, I would offer it to you, but unfortunately we have none." We discussed whether the Koran really prohibited drinking for a few minutes, and then Sayyid Ben Alim suggested we start our lesson. "And where is Susan? Surely she must learn our language, too?" I told him she was very busy with her classes now but did intend to join our classes later. This time Mr. Ben Alim seemed angry, but we had our lesson anyway. He left an hour later, promising to return the next week.

By this time I was not sure I wanted to continue with the lessons. We spoke little Arabic, and I did not want to be put in the position of violating Libyan law by serving alcohol. I also wondered about his interest in my wife.

Country: Mexico

Issue: Favors Through Contacts; How to Get Things Done

Source: Unknown

Mr. Jensen collapsed into a chair. "I cannot understand all this red tape," he said, scratching his head. "You would not believe what I have been through the past few days."

Mr. Lopez smiled sympathetically.

Jensen continued: "I went out to the university in the morning to get permission to look at the special collection of documents. You remember I told you that I need to see them for this study on New World archaeology that I am doing. But do you think I could get anywhere near them?"

"I was sent to the archaeology department and sat in the office until they finally sent me to the admissions office. I stood in line for forty-five minutes, then they did not know what to do with me and sent me to the library. I waited over an hour at the library for a Mr. Something-or-other, who finally came to say that he could not help me without permission from someone over in the anthropology department—and on and on. I walked all over that campus and talked to a dozen secretaries, and I am no further now than I was when I started!"

He shook his head and let his hands drop into his lap. "I just don't know where to go next."

Lopez smiled. "I know how it is. Well, I cannot promise I can do anything, but I have a friend in the political science department. Maybe he can help."

"Political science? But I'm working on archaeology."

"Well, we will see."

The next day the two men drove to the university. They walked quickly to the political science offices, and Mr. Lopez disappeared for a few minutes. Soon he reappeared with another man, whom he introduced as Mr. Alvarez. They shook hands and talked for a few minutes, and then Mr. Jensen explained the study he was working on and his need to see some of the documents in the archaeology collection.

"Well," said Mr. Alvarez, "I think I can help you. One of the professors in that department is a good friend of mine. Why don't you come back in about an hour?"

In an hour they were back in Mr. Alvarez's office.

"Go on over to the archaeology department," he said. "They are expecting you and will be happy to show you their documents collection."

They thanked Mr. Alvarez warmly, and the two men left. As they walked across the campus, Jensen asked in amazement, "Now how could he do in an hour what I could not accomplish in several days?"

Area:	Mid-East (General)
Issue:	Indirect Approach vs. Direct Approach
Source:	Unknown

Jabar was having difficulties at home. His wife was ill and had been for some time. His brother's wife had quarreled with her and now refused to help out with the children, and his mother had gone to the provinces to visit his sister and her husband. There was really no one to take care of the children. In addition to this, his brother had gotten himself into some difficulties with the tax collectors and so he had loaned him a large sum of money, which left him with very little for his own family. In short, he was having trouble making ends meet. He has taken another job at night to try to get a little more money, but this was very wearing because now he had no time to sleep.

Some months before, his wife had been walking down the street when she saw a little girl fall and hurt herself. She helped the little girl, comforted her, and took her home. She was the daughter of his boss and his boss had been very grateful to him for what his wife had done. Jabar decided to go to see his boss about his present difficulties and he hoped that his boss would be able to do something for him. So late one afternoon he went to his boss.

"Good afternoon, Modir Sayb, how does the day find you? Are you well? Are you fine? Is your health good? Is your family well? Are you fine, thanks to God?"

"Good afternoon, Jabar. How are you? How is your family? How is your health? Are you well? Yes, we are all well, thanks be to God. Please sit down. It gives me great pleasure to see you. Will you have some tea? Xo, baccha, bring tea for us. Please sit here. Are you comfortable?"

"Thank you very much, Modir Sayb. You shouldn't trouble yourself for me. I am fine here. I am very grateful to you. You really shouldn't trouble yourself." "So, Jabar, I hope life is treating you well? We are very fortunate this year to have had a good spring rain but I am certainly glad it has finally stopped. So much mud! It was difficult. Always so much mud!" "Yes, sayb. That is true. It must have been very difficult for you. But now it is over and we have a good summer ahead of us."

"Ah, yes. Allah is good. Well, here is the tea. No, not on that table, put it on this table. Good. Please excuse the boy. He is very lazy and stupid, but he is honest. One cannot expect everything from these people." "That is true. I hope that your family is well?" "Oh yes, it is good of you to ask. Karim is a fine student at the university and little Shala will be starting school next spring." "It is indeed a great honor for Karim to go to the university. You must be very proud of him." "Yes, indeed. If he does well enough he may be able to go abroad to study. That would be very good for him. I am seeing now what I can do about it." "Oh, I am sure there will not be any problems for you, Sayb. You are very fortunate." "Thank you, Jabar. Fortunate praises to Allah." "And little Shala. What a fine daughter. A credit to her family. I hope she hasn't fallen and hurt herself again?" "Well, you know how it is with young children. She is very fond of you and asks about you often. And you, Jabar? I trust all is well with you?" "Oh yes, Modir Sayb. We are fortunate that I have such a good job. Indeed Sir, we are most indebted to you. We are having some illness now and a little difficulty, but it is not great, I assure you, and will quickly pass, Enshallah." "Yes, we all have difficult times, sad to say. Please have some more tea?" "Thank you, Sir, you are most kind and generous." "You need not worry about anything." "Thank you, Modir Sayb. And thank you for the tea. Good-bye."

Country: North Africa

Issue: Problem of Being a Single Woman

Source: *Letters from North Africa*, ed. by Gordon Schimmel, Volunteer Liaison Officer, Division of Volunteer Support. Division of University Relations and Training and the Office of Programming and Planning. Peace Corps 1966.

My roommate and I teach at a boarding school. The students are well-disciplined, and there has never been any question as to my authority, either in class or after hours. I'm paid all the respect I could possibly expect. I have a good image, and I suspect that my presence there has done more good than harm.

As a part of the community, however, the value of my presence is highly questionable. Typical host country nationals who learn that I live alone with another girl, am single, and teach at a boys' school, suffer absolute misunderstanding. What bad thing did she do, that she was sent here? Why isn't she married? Is something wrong with her? Obviously from a very bad family. What kind of parents would allow this? And gone to school, too! I notice she has a number of visitors, all of them men. And she blatantly looks you in the face as she buys your onions. Such disgraceful dress. Thank God we keep our women in their place—at home.

I can't fight being thought of as a prostitute. How does one prove she's not a witch? Nearly everything I do to disprove them has the opposite effect. Suppose I meet an employee at the airline office and he invites me to his house, and I accept. I hope to meet an entire family and, perhaps, on the outside, establish the beginnings of a rewarding friendship. But the men in the office understand—they know the conditions of my invitations much better than I, and I've only reinforced what they've thought all along. Oblivious, I drag my roommate along to meet what we both are sure will be a typical host country family, as was promised. We find ourselves in a room with two other men. When we ask to see the women, they come in briefly, talk little, and soon leave. The evening drags on. When we leave, our hands are squeezed, even kissed and we're invited back for the next night. As we back out, the bulbs in our heads suddenly brighten, and we are appalled to realize that we've led them on.

Women are sealed off from us. We have precious few chances to meet them, and then it's usually through a husband, which gets us off on the wrong foot immediately. I can just about count on being considered a potential mistress by both the man and his wife. Whether I'm an undesireable companion, whether wives don't want me making a fool of myself and their husbands, or whether they would like to know me, I don't know. I rather suspect that they care very little about seeing me after an initial curiosity because my pattern of living is far outside their range of experience or possibility. I fetch about the same interest as a baby gorilla—fascinating, but a monster, nevertheless.

Country: North Africa

Issue: The Expectations that Indigenous People have of Americans

Source: *Letters from North Africa*, ed. by Gordon Schimmel, Volunteer Liaison Officer, Division of Volunteer Support. Division of University Relations and Training and the Office of Programming and Planning. The Peace Corps. 1966

An official of the Ministry of Education visited my secondary school, and noticed that the PCVs located at the school were riding bicycles to school while the host counry teachers and expatriots were riding *Mobylettes*, scooters, and some were even arriving in cars.

Later he commented to me that he thought it would be more appropriate for me to make use of similar transportation, rather than to appear each morning riding on bikes like schoolboys.

I explained that it is Peace Corps policy that we not own a motorized vehicle, and we are encouraged to use bicycles since we live a good distance from the school.

He replied that this was unrealistic and foolish. "Everyone," he says, "expects Americans to own *cars!* Didn't the Americans invent the car?"

I answered him by saying, "If PCVs owned scooters or cars, it would remove them from the level of the ordinary North Africans, and we would begin to appear like 'ugly Americans.' "

"You are not like ordinary North Africans", he stated, "You are professional people hired by the government to do a job. And the government expects efficiency from you, not acrobatics on bikes."

Country: North Africa

Issue: Requests for Financial Aid

Source: *Letters From North Africa*, ed. by Gordon Schimmel, Volunteer Liaison Officer, Division of Volunteer Support. Division of University Relations and Training and the Office of Programming and Planning. Peace Corps. 1966.

The term has just ended at the school where you are teaching when one of the boys who has been in your class approaches you. The student has done well in his studies and is especially eager to learn. He asks if he could speak to you in private about a very serious matter. You invite him to your house and sit down to talk. The boy tells you how much he has enjoyed being in your class the previous term and how he is looking forward to being in your class the coming term. He stresses how much education means to him and how much he appreciates the fact that you are helping to improve his chance for obtaining an education.

Finally, the boy comes to the specific reason for his visit: his father refuses to pay his school fees for the coming term. According to his father, he has had enough education and it is time that he go to work to help him make a living for the rest of the family. He is now able to read and write...and that is enough. The father says he cannot afford to pay for more education than that.

The boy states that because his father will not pay his school fees, he has no choice but to ask you for the money, which he needs if he is to continue his education.

Country: North Africa

Issue: Pressure to Socialize vs. American Drive to Work and Produce

Source: *Letters from North Africa*, ed. by Gordon Schimmel, Volunteer Liaison Officer, Division of Volunteer Support. Division of University Relations and Training and the Office of Programming and Planning. Peace Corps. 1966.

While sitting in a cafe with a few co-teachers you mention that you are interested in buying pottery which is produced in a nearby village and sold in the local *medina*. You explain that you have little idea where the pottery is sold, and one of the co-teachers offers to take you there.

The next day during lunch the two of you set off for the medina, and upon finding the pottery your friend proceeds to bargain for you, "so that you will get a *bon prix*,"—one lower than that which most tourists have to pay. The transaction completed, you go to a nearby cafe, drink some tea and talk over teaching experiences at school. He then suggests that you meet at the cinema the next afternoon after classes and invites you to a party which is to be held at a friend's house following the film. You accept, a bit reluctantly, knowing that you still have papers to correct and an exam to write for the end of the week.

Following the cinema the next evening, the two of you arrive to find the party well underway. A few people are playing cards or just sitting and talking, while most of the group is twisting to French versions of American rock n' roll records. The group is all male. After refusing several invitations to twist, you decide to be a sport and dance.

Upon making your effort for "the Corps" and talking for a while, you explain that it is already late and you still have papers to correct and an exam to write. Despite protests from your friend and the others, you leave assuring everyone that you enjoyed the party and would love to stay, but you simply have too much work to do.

The next day at lunch your friend informs you that he is hurt because you left the party so early and that you insulted the host by not staying until the food was served. He explains, however, that fortunately he was able to explain your departure and in spite of it all the group would like you to go to the beach with them on Sunday—the day you planned to correct the exam.

Country: Peru

Issue: Time; Activity vs. Results

Source: Brigham Young University, Language and Intercultural Research Center, Communication Learning Aid, 1977.

"Señorita, are you sure Señor Vega remembered our appointment?," Mr. Matthews asked for the second time.

"Oh, yes, I'm absolutely positive."

"But it's nearly 3:45 p.m. I've been waiting here since three o'clock," Matthews said impatiently. "Why don't you remind him?"

"He's probably just taking care of some last minute items. I'm sure he hasn't forgotten that you're waiting. He'll no doubt be free right away," said the secretary.

Mr. Matthews returned to his chair. "I guess I'd better not press the matter any further," he thought. "She seems to be getting a little upset. And why should she be put out? Who does Vega think he is anyway? I've been waiting for nearly an hour!"

He sat back and tried to concentrate on the magazine he was looking at, even though he didn't understand a word of Spanish.

He thought back to when he had first arrived in Peru. That had been nearly a month ago. He had enjoyed most of that time spent in Lima. But when he had come to the interior, things had been different.

"There are times," he thought, "when I would like to pack my bags and just not bother with this place any more. Like that work day we scheduled two weeks ago to lay bricks for the new park compound. Most of the supervisors didn't show up, and the few that did seemed to think it was beneath them to work up a sweat. And then there was that committee meeting last week. Nobody got there on time. There were people straggling in nearly an hour after the meeting was supposed to have started."

"Señor Vega will see you now," said the secretary, interrupting Mr. Matthews' thoughts.

"Thank you," responded Matthews as he entered Vega's office. "I don't know what I'm thanking her for, though," he thought. "I've *never* been treated so rudely! Who does he think I am, the paper boy?"

Country: The Philippines

Issue: Hospitality

Source: *The Peace Corps Volunteer in the Philippines*, prepared by Lone Castillo and Paul Boriack, Volumes A and B. Peace Corps.

The Paterno family has accepted you as their new daughter. They express a great deal of concern over your being well taken care of.

When you arrived, the family had a big party. The meals since have been lavish. The food is so delicious and the servings so frequent that you are rapidly gaining weight.

On several occasions you have raised the question of payment for board with Mrs. Paterno. Her reaction has varied from being slightly insulted, although good humored, to vague remarks about settling the matter by and by or that you can pay whatever you like.

Your teachers have indicated that P50.00 per month is a fair price. You offer this to Mrs. Paterno and she flatly refuses.

Country: The Philippines

Issue: Invasion of Privacy; Personal Questions

Source: Brigham Young University, Language and Intercultural Research Center, Communication Learning Aid, 1977.

"Are you all moved into your new apartment now?" Teresita asked.

"Yes. I think I'll like it a lot," Sylvia replied.

"What do you do when you finish work?" Teresita continued.

"Oh, lots of things." Sylvia was becoming annoyed.

"And does your family approve of your living alone?"

"They don't mind." Sylvia searched for a way to end the conversation quickly. "Excuse me, I must help this customer," she said, and hurried to the front of the bank.

Sylvia had been at work only two days since she transferred from the United States offices. She was doing the same type of work she'd done in America, but she found that occasionally some variations had been made in the Philippines branch procedures.

Sylvia was glad to learn the new techniques and have errors pointed out, but it seemed to her that every time Teresita, her superior, talked with her about a problem, she ended the conversation by asking personal questions.

"I hardly know her, and here she is prying into everything I do," Sylvia thought angrily. "I'll just have to tell her next time that it's none of her business."

Country: Samoa

Issue: Work Ethic; Immediate vs. Delayed Gratification

Source: Brigham Young University, Language and Intercultural Research Center, Communication Learning Aid, 1977.

A young Samoan returned to his island after graduating from an American university. Ioane Yo-ah-nay had studied agronomy at the university and was anxious to implement a plan which he thought would raise the standard of living at his small, rural village.

Ioane knew how anxious his people were to obtain some foreign goods. But since they lived largely from subsistence agriculture they had little cash. He knew that foreign goods could be more easily obtained if the villagers raised and sold a surplus of their own subsistence crops. Ioane held one of the 15 village chief titles and had the added status of an overseas education. He had enough savings to allow him to make a practical demonstration of his plan by raising some crops of his own.

At one of his first meetings with the council of chiefs, Ioane talked with the matai about the desirability of building a village store. Ioane said he would give them his savings money in return for a 100 acre clearing in the forest. This money would be sufficient for the matai to build and stock a small store.

The proposal was accepted. It was estimated that 80 men could clear the 100 acres in a week. The area for clearing was chosen and a shelter built. At the end of the week, less than four acres had been cleared. Each day the men had gone to work on their own plantations instead.

None of the matais seemed surprised or distressed. They divided the money among themselves and forgot about the store. It was some time before Ioane realized what had happened. His acquired Western enthusiasm and practicality had led him to forget that there is an inherent conflict between Western and Samoan ways of looking at life—a basic difference in what they consider most important. The chiefs really wanted to obtain some foreign goods, but they found it more practical to use the money Ioane paid them to buy some goods now than to plan for the future revenues a store might produce.

Country:	Spain
Issue:	Male-Female Roles
Source:	Brigham Young University Language and Intercultural Research Center, Communication Aid, 1977

Phyllis dropped behind the group to take another look at Velazquez' *Las Meniñas.* She needed more time to enjoy the excitement of seeing the fascinating masterpiece in person. Besides, she felt restricted and a little childish tromping through the Prado Museum with the other American students, flitting from painting to painting like a swarm of tourists. She was startled to hear a voice, almost in her ear, ask, "You like the picture?" She turned to see a very good-looking young Spaniard smiling down at her. He was nicely dressed, and though his English was accented, it was understandable. He seemed obviously educated and very eager to strike up a conversation.

"It's just marvelous!" she responded, "more beautiful than I had ever imagined."

The young man smiled with pleasure and then smoothly and

agressively led her through a series of questions about who she was, what she was doing in Spain, how long and where she was staying.

Phyllis was flattered by his attention and interest and gave him her fullest smile and wittiest answers in return. She had just wondered if she should invite him to her dorm, when suddenly the harsh voice of her Spanish Art Instructor broke in.

"Venga, Señorita! Come with the group, please! We are waiting for you and have no time for you to talk to strangers."

Embarrassed, Phyllis hastily said goodbye to the young man and followed her teacher, who seemed furious that she had been so friendly with the young man.

"You should not be so receptive to that kind of person," he stormed. "He was picking you up like a common street tramp."

Phyllis turned crimson. "Like a what?" She stammered, "I thought he was just being very nice."

"You Americans are so naive," replied the professor. "Any Spanish girl would have immediately recognized that he was just out to gratify his male ego with another conquest. Men are like that."

Country: Thailand

Issue: Saving Face

Source: Brigham Young University, Language and Intercultural Research Center, Communication Learning Aid, 1977

Mike had asked the tour group to wait for him while he returned to take some more pictures of the floating market. But when he returned to the bus stop, the group had left him behind.

He knew the tour was going next to Jim Thompson's Thai house, an art and handicrafts museum. He decided to ask directions and see if he could catch up with them there.

Mike approached a distinguished-looking man who emerged from an office building carrying a briefcase. When he discovered the man could speak some English, he asked directions to the Thai House.

The man told Mike how to get to the museum and even suggested a bus he could take. But to Mike's dismay, when he got off the bus it was obvious he had been directed to the wrong place.

Mike was angry with himself that he had trusted the Thai man to understand his English. "But, I thought he spoke English very well," Mike thought to himself. "If he didn't understand, why would he have given me the wrong directions?"

Country: Thailand

Issue: The Patriarchal Family

Source: Brigham Young University, Language and Intercultural Research Center, Communication Learning Aid, 1977.

Helen was the daughter of an American businessman who supervised the establishment of a new business in Thailand. Her family lived in Thailand for a year. Some of the first friends she made were Naiyana and her sister Niramon.

When she first visited their home, Helen was introduced to Mr. and Mrs. Chaimongkol and to a younger brother, Damrong. Also living with the family was Mr. Chaimongkol's father. When Helen's family lived in the United States, her grandparents did not live nearby. Occasionally they visited Helen's family. The older woman was loved and respected, but was generally treated as a guest in the home.

One of the first adjustments Helen had to make to the Thai culture was the custom of grandparents living with families, which, it seemed to her, only compounded their crowded living conditions. She was even more surprised to learn that the grandfather was actually considered the family head and that his opinion was always sought in important decisions.

Helen remembered, for instance, how on one occasion she was visiting with Naiyana when the father came home from work. He was enthusiastic about a new opportunity for a business investment which he had just learned about. He sought out his father and related the details of the venture to him. After some deliberation, the grandfather stated that he did not think the investment a wise decision. To Helen's amazement Mr. Chaimongkol accepted his father's opinion and said he wouldn't go forward with his plans.

"Maybe my dad would talk to Grandpa about an idea," Helen remarked to herself at the time, "but he sure wouldn't let Grandpa push him around. He'd make his own decision."

Country: Turkey

Issue: Male-Female Relationships

Source: *A Case Study of Teaching in Turkey: Some Problems Faced by Peace Corps Volunteers.* Prepared by the International Research Institute of the American Institutes for Research, 1966.

When we got back to town a little before noon, I suggested

that we take Karen out to lunch. Guy answered, "She's working today, but she knows you're coming to town. Why don't you drop by the hospital? I'll clean up some errands I have to do and see you back at the apartment around two o'clock.

Karen was pleased to see me when I got to the hospital and arranged to take her lunch break right away. When I invited her out to lunch, she explained that she didn't lunch in public with men except with a group of people. She didn't even see Guy unless he came up to the hospital or they were both invited to someone's house. So we ate at the hospital cafeteria. "Aren't you being overly cautious?," I asked. "Carsi is a pretty big town, or seems to be compared to Kucukyer."

"I don't know. Maybe," she answered. "People gossip a lot here, even more than in the little town I grew up in back home. In a big city it probably wouldn't matter, but here I do feel I have to be accepted by the women of the town so that they'll listen to my advice. I used to think I was being too careful, until a few days ago when I got a letter from Mary telling me what happened to Sue.

"Sue's teaching in a town bigger than Carsi, isn't she?" I asked.

"Yes, quite a lot bigger," Karen answered. "It seems incredible that so much should be made of so little. According to Mary, Sue only dated a Turkish teacher a few times. They went to a play or concert and met for coffee a couple of times. The next thing Sue knew, the Turk was spending all his time checking up on her. Everywhere she went, there he was."

"She must have been annoyed, but what was so disturbing about it?" I asked, thinking that Sue could have explained to him that he was being too possessive.

"Disturbing!" Karen repeated wryly. "That's the understatement of the year! Accepting the attention of a young man here is a serious thing. Then appearing to reject him—he's humiliated. And of course, everybody in town knows about it and talks about it. Sue's friend created awful scenes. That made an impossible situation for her at school and even hurt Mary's standing with some of the teachers who didn't know them very well. It got so serious that the Rep had to be called in. He was still there when Mary wrote to me, and they hadn't decided what to do. So you see," she concluded, "I'd rather be overly cautious, as you put it, than take the chance of getting into a nasty situation. Imagine having to leave your town when you'd only just gotten started."

"You must spend a lot of time alone then," I said, not quite sure whether Karen wanted sympathy or not.

"Alone! Are you kidding?" she exclaimed. "I'm almost never alone. Finding time to wash my hair is a big problem. But don't think I'm griping. The women on the staff and in the town are really trying to help me feel at home."

I got the point. "You mean all those invitations that you really don't have time to accept, but can't refuse?"

"That's it," she said. "And, from what Guy tells me, it's a little more complicated for women than for men. Do you know about the *Gun?*"

"No, what's a *Gun?*"

"A *Gun* is something like a ladies' tea back home," Karen explained. "About a month ago I really goofed when... Oh, I'd better describe it from the beginning. Before, I'd always gone with a Turkish friend, but that day I went alone. As fate would have it, I arrived a little late and most of the women had already greeted the hostess and were seated in the customary circle. Well, I started around the circle, shaking hands with each woman and repeating the formal greeting that you use at a *Gun*. I was nearly at the end of the circle and was beginning to think I'd done a pretty good job when I goofed. With some women you're supposed to kiss her hand and press it to your forehead, and with some you're not supposed to. I did it when I shouldn't have. Immediately there was a little ripple of surprise. I felt like sinking through the floor."

"What did you do?"

"What could I do? I smiled apologetically and got through the greeting process as fast as I could. But I learned my lesson! Now I always arrange to go with a Turkish friend—and make sure that she precedes me around the circle!"

After lunch, Karen took me on a quick tour of the hospital. Just as I was leaving, we met Dr. Gencer, the assistant director of the hospital and Karen's supervisor. "I am very pleased to meet another of the American Volunteers for the Peace Corps," he said when Karen introduced us. "Would you and Guy *Bey* honor me with a visit to my home tomorrow night?"

I replied in what I hoped was a properly formal manner, "I would be very much honored to visit your home, if my friend has not made other plans for the evening."

As they walked with me to the door, Karen murmured, "Please try to make it. I'll be there and we may get another chance to talk. The Gencers' parties really are fun."

Country: Turkey

Issue: Classroom Discipline

Source: *A Case Study of Teaching in Turkey: Some Problems Faced by Peace Corps Volunteers.* Prepared by the International Research Institute of the American Institutes for Research, 1966.

I had arrived on a Saturday and classes began the following Monday; I really felt pushed. Although the textbook for each class contained all of the material to be presented during the year, it was left to each teacher to develop his own schedules and lesson plans. Because I wasn't really sure of either myself or my classes, planning was a hard chore and took up most of my free time. The Turks, meanwhile, were sparing no efforts to make me feel at home. Often I wished there were fewer invitations so that I could get organized and try to find out what I was doing.

As I grew more familiar with my classes, my struggles with lesson plans increased. Each class had kids with such varying preparation that I couldn't find a level that didn't seem too difficult for someone. It was hard to tell; the kids seemed shy and hesitated to volunteer answers to my questions. Although I knew the Turkish teachers were very formal in the classroom, I smiled a lot and tried to show friendly encouragement to get some response from my quiet students. I got the feeling many of them were just sitting through the classes and never did their homework. Puzzled, I asked Ekrem *Bey*, the *Lise* math teacher, how I could get some response. "When they grow accustomed to you, they will respond." he assured me. "Most of them have never seen an American before. You are strange to them."

Determined to reach the kids and capture their interest, I slaved over my lesson preparations, trying to make English interesting. Without realizing it, I was trying to run an American class in a Turkish school.

Ekrem *Bey* was right. I got response—too much of it. The first class to blow up was the second-year class at the Trade School. I'd been trying to get them to understand the purpose of the oral drills. I hadn't been able to put it across with my limited Turkish, so I had prepared visual displays showing the difficult points in each lesson. Then we'd do drills on those points. One day toward the end of the fourth week of school, as I turned away from the class to hang up the drill charts, the response came. Without any warning, everyone started talking at once.

Raping my pencil on the desk I said, "Please, let's have quiet." The sound diminished but did not stop. There were 75 students, sitting three to a desk, and I couldn't spot who was continuing the disturbance. Raising my voice over the persistent rumble, I started a drill. "The pencil is on the desk. Everyone please repeat."

A few of the kids in the front rows started to recite "The pencil is..." when a falsetto voice called out from the back of the room, "Zee peenceel ees ann zee...," deliberately distorting the vocal sounds. Like the cheering section at a football game, the kids in the back rows picked it up and chanted, "Zee peenceel ees...," while the others laughed, talked, and shoved one another's books on the floor.

I wasn't sure I knew who the original culprit was, but I couldn't let them get away with that. I called Ali Adivar, who seemed to be the leader of the cheering section, to come to the blackboard and write the drill as the rest of the class recited. Protesting, "*Hocam,* I did not do it. It was Kemal, not me," he walked slowly to the board. By the time the class ended, I had twelve kids lined up writing furiously and no room for any more, but the horseplay kept up.

One by one, each of my classes "responded." I had a battle on my hands nearly every hour. Pop quizzes, difficult questions designed to humiliate the troublemakers, lectures, threats—nothing worked. I wasn't teaching my English and it was clear that I didn't have their respect.

Finally, I sent some offenders to the *Mudar Bey's* office. This had a calming effect for a little while, but I couldn't quite take the hand-kissing apologies. Discussing the problem with the Turkish teachers wasn't too helpful either. As Ekrem *Bey* gently put it. "The flesh belongs to the teacher; the bones to the father." In short, slug the worst offenders. I found this more distasteful than having my hand kissed.

I tried to explain to Ekrem: "Hitting a student is very difficult for me. I am not criticizing your way, but I am not used to such a different method of disciplining children and I can't bring myself to do it."

He seemed to understand and replied, "If it is difficult for you, perhaps you might enlist one of the larger boys to act as your proctor. It is not uncommon for Turkish teachers to curb the trouble-makers in that way. Of course, the student would expect that his work would be viewed more kindly..." This sounded as if I would be depending on a bully; it wasn't at all appealing and I didn't try it.

One day after the second-year students at the Trade School had been unusually noisy, even for them, Hasan *Bey* came into the room. He studied my wall charts and we talked about them for a bit. Then he asked, "Are your students being more cooperative? You haven't sent any to my office lately." What could I say? "I feel silly when they kiss my hand?" I mumbled something about trying to work it out, but I don't think he doubted for a minute the real reason for my change in strategy. Fortunately, it was time for me to go over to the *Lise* for my afternoon classes, so I thanked him for his concern and escaped.

As I walked along I puzzled over what I could do. If the uproars so common in my classrooms were disrupting work in other rooms, I might not get the chance to handle the problem myself. If I didn't stop the chaos, I'd never teach anything. Was Hasan *Bey* just trying to encourage me or was he warning me? Somehow I had to do something.

The weeks dragged by. On Mondays and Thursdays I hated to get up. That was when I taught—using the word in its loosest possible sense—the Trade School second-year class. Thursdays were especially bad; I had them for a double session. Then came the week of rain. Appropriately, it started on a Thursday and poured down all day without letup. My apartment was cold and damp and there was mildew in the closet. All my shoes were wet and even though I stuffed them with newspaper and singed them on the wood stove, the insides did not dry out. My bed felt like a slab in the morgue.

At ten o'clock on the eighth day of rain, I collided with the second-year class. For fifteen minutes I had been trying to get their attention. No longer was I smiling at them encouraging them; I just wanted them to keep quiet. Kemal, who really wasn't such a bad kid, had finally gotten the hang of a new sound and had been chanting, to himself, "Blue, blue, blue," over and over. I'd just convinced him to stop and practice later when Ali Adivar, who sat directly in front of my desk where I could keep an eye on him, began, "Blue-ue-ue-ue-, Blue-ue-ue..." It was funny; nonetheless, when the class roared with laughter, something snapped. I pulled Ali out of his chair and shook him. He sidled back to his seat. Turning to face the class, I found, to my amazement, a look of respect in their eyes. It seemed to say, "Well, you've finally wised up!"

I didn't feel wised up, I felt depressed and I couldn't stop my knees and voice from shaking. But the remainder of the class hour did go surprisingly well.

Resource 11
"AS IF..." EXERCISE

Divide the group into pairs or triads, and assign each to consider in detail what a society would be like if it were based on one of the premises listed below. Allow twenty minutes, then regroup and report to the entire group, eliciting additional comments from others as well.

What would a society be like if it believed implicitly—
1. in reincarnation and karma
2. that all other people are infidels
3. that all events in the world are determined by Fate
4. a person's worth is determined solely by his/her "high" birth
5. in the passive approach to life as preferable to an action orientation
6. that certain ethnic or racial groups are intellectually inferior and emotionally immature
7. that old people are to be revered, honored and deferred to in all instances
8. that aesthetic values are of supreme importance and should be used to determine every major issue in life
9. that rights of groups are more important than those of the individual
10. that women are superior to men

Final points to be made at the end of the discussion:
- There *are*, or have been, groups or societies which believe all of these premises and shape their lives around them.
- *And most of these premises are very "un-American" (ie.,* except for #6, American society tends to be based on premises which are diametrically opposed to those listed above).

Resource 12

INTERCULTURAL HYPOTHESES

1. Human beings are creators of culture.
2. Each group developed its own culture, thousands of years ago, in isolation.
3. Each group found its own ways to solve mankind's ten basic problems:

• Food	• Government
• Clothing	• War/Protection
• Shelter	• Arts/Crafts
• Family Organization	• Knowledge/Science
• Social Organization	• Religion

4. It is inevitable that different groups would develop different solutions to these ten problems.
5. There are no absolutely "right" responses—only "right" or "wrong" responses *within* any given culture. One culture is not "better" or "worse"—only *different* from another.
6. However, each culture *thinks* its own ways are superior (= ethnocentricity).
7. All children raised into a particular culture are *enculturated* into that culture's "right" ways.
8. There is no problem of a cross-cultural nature when a person stays in his/her own culture.
9. Problems of an intercultural nature occur when a person who has been enculturated into one culture is suddenly dumped into another very different culture, or when a person of one culture tries to communicate with a person of another culture.

Resource 13
FOR FURTHER READING...

Popular ↑

Scholarly ↓

- *Intercultural Communicating.* Language Research Center, Brigham Young University. Provo, Utah: 1976.
- *Survival Kit for Overseas Living.* L. Robert Kohls, Intercultural Press, 70 West Hubbard Street, Chicago: 1979.
- *Learning About Peoples and Cultures.* Seymour Fersh, ed. McDougal, Littell & Co. Evanston, Illinois: 1974.
- *The Silent Language.* Edward T. Hall. Doubleday. Garden City,New York: 1959.
- *An Introduction to Intercultural Communication.* John C. Condon and Fathai Yousef. Bobbs-Merrill. Indianapolis: 1975.
- *Understanding Intercultural Communication.* Larry Samovar, Richard E. Porter and Nemi C. Jain. Wadsworth Publishing Company. Belmont, California: 1981.
- *Intercultural Communication: A Reader* (second edition). Larry A. Samovar and Richard E. Porter. Wadsworth Publishing Company. Belmont, California: 1981.

Practical

Business

- *All You Need to Know About Living Abroad.* Eleanor R. Pierce. Doubleday (for Pan American World Airways). New York, latest edition.
- *Living Overseas.* Louise Winfield. Public Affairs Press. Washington, D.C.: 1962.
- *Managing Cultural Differences.* Philip R. Harris and Robert T. Moran. Gulf Publishing Company. Houston, Texas: 1979.

INTERCULTURAL COMMUNICATION BIBLIOGRAPHIES

- The best general bibliography is included in Condon and Yousef: *An Introduction to Intercultural Communication*, Bobbs-Merrill Company. Indianapolis: 1975.

- Seelye, H. Ned and V. Lynn Tyler. *Intercultural Communicator Resources*. Language and Intercultural Research Center of Brigham Young University. Provo. Utah: 1977.

- SIETAR (The Society for Intercultural Education, Training and Research) eventually plans to publish an extensive bibliography which will be computerized. Printouts of specialized sub-fields will be available for a small fee from SIETAR, 1414 Twenty-second Street, NW, Washington, D.C. 20037.

- The Bridge, a quarterly review of cross-cultural affairs and international training, published by the Center for Research and Education (a division of the Systran Corporation), 1800 Pontiac Street, Denver, Colorado 80220, is the best up-to-date source of more recent publications in this field. Current items can be purchased directly from their bookstore.

AREA STUDIES RESOURCES

- *Country Studies* (formerly *Area Handbooks*)
  Foreign Area Studies Group at American University.
  Available from the Superintendent of Documents, U.S.
  Government Printing Office, Washington, D.C.   20402.
  Country Studies available for 108 countries.

- *Country Updates*
  Alison Lanier
    from Intercultural Press, 70 West Hubbard Street,
      Chicago, Illinois   60610
  Country Updates available for 22 countries

- Knowledge Industry Publications
  2 Corporate Park Drive
  White Plains, New York   10604
    "Overseas Assignment Directory Service"
    Information on 37 countries.

- Price-Waterhouse & Company
  1251 Avenue of the Americas
  New York, New York   10020
    "Information Guide for Doing Business in_____"
    Information on 48 countries.

- Multinational Business Center
  World-Wide Business Centers
  575 Madison Avenue,   Suite 1006
  New York, New York   10022
  Multinational Executive Travel Companion
  Covering 160 countries.

- The Language and Intercultural Research Center
  Brigham Young University   240, B-34
  Provo, Utah   84602
  "Culturgrams" for 70 countries.
  "Building Bridges of Understanding with the People of
  _____" for 11 countries.

- "Background Notes" for 157 countries.
  Available from the Superintendent of Documents, U.S.
  Government Printing Office, Washington, D.C.   20402.

- Center for Area and Country Studies
  The Foreign Service Institute
  U.S. Department of State
  1400 Key Boulevard
  Arlington, Virginia   20520
  Publishes excellent bibliographies for eight geographic
  regions of the world.

- Pleasant Valley Press
  Friends of History
  Thorn Hill Industrial Park
  125 Commonwealth Drive
  Warrendale, Pennsylvania   15086
  Publishes *Cultures and Peoples of the World* volumes for:
  - Arab World
  - Oceania and Philippines
  - Central America
  - Black Africa
  - Northern Europe
  - Indonesia
  - South America
  - Western Asia
  - North America
  - Southern Europe
  - India
  - Central and East Asia

- "Bibliographic Surveys" (annotated bibliographies)
  Prepared by the Department of the Army for ten militarily
  strategic regions.
  Available from the Superintendent of Documents, U.S.
  Government Printing Office, Washington, D.C.   20402
- *All You Need to Know About Living Abroad.*
  Eleanor R. Pierce
  Published by Doubleday for Pan American World Airways.
  Logistical information on 93 countries; latest edition.
- *Living in Europe*
  Alison R. Lanier.
  Published by Scribner's Sons, New York; latest edition.
  Logistical information on the major European countries.
- Human Relations Area Files
  755 Prospect Street
  New Haven, Connecticut
  Provides access to voluminous entries of anthropological
  nature on all the cultures and sub-cultures of the world. For
  the really serious student, copies of the file are also housed in
  twenty universities across the U.S.
- Many American libraries now have access to computerized
  bibliographic banks which can, in short order and at minimal
  cost, produce an annotated bibliography on the country of your interest.

ADDITIONAL EXERCISES AND RESOURCES

The basic workshop (as indicated in the Lesson Plan, pp. xvii through ix) may be expanded by the addition of any number of auxiliary exercises. Several are included in this book. Feel free to substitute or add any of these or other exercises with which you may be familiar.

Among those additional exercises which are included in this book are:

- *Resource 2:* Cross-Cultural Value Cards
  Instructions are included with the resource itself. This makes a good initial activity and, as such, may be substituted for Resource 1, or it may be used in addition to the other exercises if time permits.

- *Resource 7:* Minoria-Majoria Simulation
  This full-group activity requires a minimum of two and one-half hours to complete (including the processing and debriefing session which should follow). For this reason, it has not been included in the Lesson Plan for the Basic Workshop, but it does make a valuable addition if time is no problem.

- *Resource 10:* Additional Case Studies
  This collection of short case studies may be adapted and used as appropriate. The reader will note that most of the case studies included as Resource 10 are from two sources: The Peace Corps and Brigham Young University. [10] In both cases, only the tip of the iceberg is exposed in this book. Many, many, more excellent cases are available from these institutions. Several useful short cases may also be found in *Some Resources for Area Training*.[11]

  Another appealing case study which should not be overlooked is "Much Depends on What We Assume: A Bank in Bogota" by Raymond Gorden. [12]

---

[10] The ACTION Library at 806 Connecticut Avenue, NW, Washington, DC, while not intended to serve the general public, has endless resources from their many training programs, and they have been most generous in sharing their riches. Brigham Young University (Language and Intercultural Research Center, 240-B-34, Provo, UT 84602) has developed a number of programmed case studies for their useful *Building Bridges of Understanding* publications.

[11] by Robert J. Foster and David T. O'Nan (Human Resources Research Office, 300 North Washington Street, Alexandria, VA 22314) 1967.

In Resource 10 disproportionate emphasis has been given to the non-Western Third World. This has been done simply because that is where the greatest contrast to the U.S. is to be found.

- *Resource 11:* "As If..." Exercise
  This exercise should only be used when the audience is a highly intellectual one.

- *Resource 12:* Intercultural Hypotheses
  Makes a good handout and, in this respect, can be used as an optional summary of some of the main points which ought to have been learned in the workshop. It works equally well as a lecturette (accompanied with an overhead projector) to summarize these very elementary but essential points.

Several excellent films may be incorporated into the workshop to stimulate discussions. Jean Marie Ackermann[13] is the best source of information on the availability of appropriate cross-cultural films. Some of the classic films which are worthy of using over and over again are:

- *Dead Birds*
  An ethnographic study of the Dani people of western New Guinea which will raise unanswerable questions for even the most intellectual audience.

- *Ceremony*
  This sensitive Japanese film presents the eternal conflict between the old and the new in an engaging, provocative manner which is sure to eliciit much self-examination and a great deal of stimulating discussion.

- *The World of Apu*
  The Satyjit Ray trilogy brings home the reality of India in a sympathetic, touching way.

- *Walkabout*
  A portrayal of life among the Aborigines in the Austrailian "outback."

- *Axe Fight*
  Deals with social conflict among the Yamomano Indians of Venezuela.

---

[12] in Fersh, S. (Ed.) *Learning About Peoples and Cultures.* McDougal, Littel & Company, Evanston, Illinois: 1974.

[13] see Ackermann, J.M. *Changing World: A Critical International Guide* (2 vols). Society for International Development, Washington, DC: 1972 and 1976.

- *Phantom India*
  An impressinistic and humanistic interpretatin of an exotic culture.

- *Bwana Toshi*
  Opportunities, discouragement, and cultural confusion face a Japanese volunteeer trying to work in an East African Setting.

- *Doing Business in Japan*
  Observes specific cultural differences in negotiation between Americans and Japanese.

The reader with a knowledge of the intercultural field may be surprised to discover that there is no mention throughout this book of the phenomenon known as "culture shock." (It is my feeling that this subject should only be included in the workshop if the participants are actually preparing to live overseas. Otherwise, it is too frightening and so theoretical as to be useless. For those with an ongoing assignment, information on culture shock and how to live through it (which could become the basis for a lecturette) may be found in the author's *Survival Kit for Overseas Living*, cited earlier. The "return culture shock" phenomenon, experienced when sojourners return to their own country, is addressed in *Coming Home Again—Return Shock*, one of Brigham Young University's "Infograms." (Available from the source cited in Resource 13, p. 66).

The final suggestion for additional activities is a videotape cassette of an encounter between Mr. Khan, an unidentified foreigner, and an American. It is excellent for analyzing cultural differences, and is available from Stephen J. Anspacher, Post Office Box 6034, Mid-City Station, Washington, D.C. 20005.

EVALUATION

To evaluate the effectiveness of the presentation of this module, a number of approaches are suggested, the first one being more conventional than the remaining examples.

Participant Rating Form

1. A simple participant rating form, administered at the end of the training, program, is the type of evaluation which is familiar to most trainers. It must be pointed out, however, that this approach can be expected to do little more than provide a rough measure of the "satisfaction level" of those who took part in the training program. Yet for your purposes, that may suffice.

The form which follows should require no more than 15 or 20 minutes for each trainee to complete. Except for the last couple of items (which are open-ended) a check placed in the appropriate place is all that is required; the results can be tallied very easily and a considerable amount of useful information provided in very short order. It is also a simple matter to compare one particular iteration of the course with any other.

After the form is administered, the items on page one should be tallied on a master sheet on which all the individual participants' scores are placed. Then circle the category with the majority of votes to obtain an overall consensus reading for each exercise.

The following form has been developed and validated by Alan Kotok.

FEEDBACK FORM

Please answer the following questions so we can learn your reactions to this program to help us prepare future programs of this type. Most questions require only an "X" in the appropriate space. You need not sign your name. Many thanks for your help.

How would you rate this program overall?

☐ Excellent ☐ Good ☐ Only fair ☐ Poor

Did this program meet

☐ All your expectations?
☐ Most of your expectations?
☐ Some of your expectations?
☐ None of your expectations?

In your opinion, did the program contain

☐ Too much material for the time allotted?
☐ About the right amount of material?
☐ Not enough material—too many sessions dragged.

How would you rate the administration of this program?

☐ Excellent—the program ran smoothly from start to finish.
☐ Good—most aspects of the program ran smoothly.
☐ Fair—only a few aspects of the program ran smoothly.
☐ Poor—no aspects of the program ran smoothly.

Please rate the following individual sessions:

Session/Trainer	Excellent	Good	Fair	Poor
Intercultural Introductions	☐	☐	☐	☐
Consensus Exercise	☐	☐	☐	☐
"Civilized"/"Primitive" Lecturette	☐	☐	☐	☐
Kluckhohn Model Presentation	☐	☐	☐	☐
American Teaching in Afghanistan Case Study	☐	☐	☐	☐
Observations by Foreign Visitors	☐	☐	☐	☐
Stereotypes of Americans by Foreigners	☐	☐	☐	☐
Discovering American Values through Proverbs	☐	☐	☐	☐
American Implicit Cultural Assumptions	☐	☐	☐	☐
Suggestions for Further Reading	☐	☐	☐	☐
Group's Analysis of Main Points	☐	☐	☐	☐

[Plus any additional activities and
minus any exercises not actually
included—in the exact sequence in
which they were presented.]

Please comment on those sessions you rated particularly high or low:

What should be done to improve this program in the future?

Please return this form to:

_____

_____

_____

_____

VARIATIONS ON THE EVALUATION PROCESS

Several more creative approaches to evaluation may challenge both the trainer and the trainees.

One technique may be to do something like this:

2. Before the workshop begins, the facilitator should handpick three participants who have the background, experience and maturity (but who do not necessarily have prior content knowledge of this subject to qualify them to evaluate the workshop) and give them the assignment of evaluating the workshop. They need be given no further instructions, other than to evaluate the trainer(s), the exercises, and the workshop's attainment of the stated objectives. So long as they achieve these ends, they may do the job in any way they decide.

Several other freer approaches are outlined in the March 1980 issue of the *Bulletin on Training.*[14] These include:

3. Divide the total training group into three equal parts and assign each team the task of suggesting ways to improve one of the following aspects of the training program: the course content, the training methodology, and the logistical arrangements. Each of these small groups should then report orally to the whole group.

4. Divide the group into pairs or triads and assign each sub-group the task of coming up with two suggestions for improving the training program. These ideas should then be shared with the whole group while someone captures all the comments on a flip chart.

5. Form a circle and have each trainee tell one thing they have learned from the course, allowing the group to add its comments as each point is made.

Finally, the reader is referred to George Renwick's excellent *Evaluation Handbook for Cross-Cultural Training and Multicultural Education*[15] for deriving your own appropriate evaluation approach.

---

[14] Published by BNA Communications, Inc., Rockville, MD 20850.

[15] Published by Intercultural Press, 70 West Hubbard Street, Chicago, IL 60610.